Moderating to
the MAX!

OTHER MARKETING BOOKS FROM PMP

MODERATING to the M.A.X.

A full-tilt guide to creative, insightful focus groups and depth interviews

$\varepsilon = mc^2$

Jean Bystedt, Siri Lynn, and Deborah Potts, Ph.D.

Illustrated by
Gregg Fraley

PARAMOUNT MARKET PUBLISHING, INC.

Paramount Market Publishing, Inc.
301 S. Geneva Street, Suite 109
Ithaca, NY 14850
www.paramountbooks.com
Telephone: 607-275-8100; 888-787-8100   Facsimile: 607-275-8101

Publisher: James Madden
Editorial Director: Doris Walsh

Cataloging in Publication Data available
ISBN 0-9725290-1-2

Contents

Acknowledgements

Many thanks are due the wonderful people who supported us in the writing of this book.

First, we thank RIVA Training Institute for its support and encouragement, especially Naomi Henderson and Grace Fuller. Prior to writing this book, we created a course and training manual called "Qualitative Toolbox" for the RIVA Training Institute. *Moderating to the Max* has been enriched by the teaching of that course, and by our contact with the many superb trainers and students with whom we've worked at RIVA.

Friends and colleagues have been there for us, as we have honed our own skills and best practices through the years. We've had the good fortune of being able to share and trade ideas with many qualitative researchers about ways to handle various situations, tools, and techniques, including those we've encountered in QRCA (Qualitative Research Consultants' Association). We thank them sincerely for their support of this book. A number of close colleagues deserve particular thanks—Diane Fraley, Linda Haviland, Elizabeth Monroe-Cook, Nancy Myers, Maureen Olsen, and Maryanne Pflug.

Thanks to all the participants in our studies, who have opened their minds and hearts to us, helping us learn more about them and, in the process, more about moderating and obtaining meaningful insights.

To Anne Pici for doing a first edit of the manuscript, and holding our hands through the myriad of bullets, semi-colons and ellipses.

Of course we thank our families for putting up with us over the past year—Gretchen, Britt, Mark, Ann, Bernie, Danica, Jaclyn, Devin, Craig, Scott, Dane, Mom, Dad, cousins, aunts, uncles. Also assorted babysitters, kindergarten teachers, yoga instructors, hairdressers, Rover, Mittens . . . STOP THE BUBBLE MACHINE! Our apologies . . . we seem to have watched one too many award programs.

But wait, one more from-the-heart (okay, sappy) thanks. We'd like to give a group hug to each other, our co-authors. The writing of this book was truly a partnership. We each brought special expertise, and are much enriched by the collaboration.

Lastly—and vitally—we thank Max and Max's creator Gregg Fraley who kept us smiling, chortling, chuckling and frankly laughing out loud during the final months of working on this book. Thanks Max, here's to you for sparking our best.

JEAN BYSTEDT
SIRI LYNN
DEBORAH POTTS
APRIL 2003

Introduction

(Or: Taking it to the Max!)

Welcome to our book. We're glad you came! Take any seat you'd like, preferably not one with any of our name cards in front of them—unless, of course, *you'd* like to moderate this session! Relax and enjoy. In these pages, we offer you tools and techniques for use in focus groups and in-depth interviews that take you beyond basic Q&A. These tools will help participants get better in touch with their own thoughts, feelings and behaviors; help them go deeper, wider and higher; help them access not just the rational but also the emotional; help them articulate and express their points of view more fully than through straight question and answer interviews. Moreover, these tools have the added benefit of keeping respondents engaged and focused. So here it is—a guide to how we think, how we do, and in some cases how we feel about a whole bunch of qualitative research tools and techniques, based on a collective 75 years of experience in the field. In fact, we're so weathered we can even remember Wolensak reel-to-reel tape recorders, writing our reports on yellow legal pads, and backrooms without M&M's! Strongly grounded in our rich experiences, we are committed to the on-going advancement of ourselves and our industry, and we look forward to the continued evolution of the field of qualitative research. We hope that this book contributes to the process.

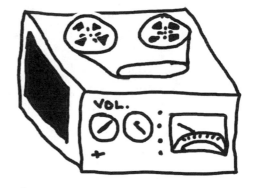

CIRCA 1971

This book is for you if . . .

> If you're a relatively **new moderator** in the field of qualitative research, this book will teach you about all those techniques

your clients are asking you to use. And because you may be wondering if you're doing them "right," we offer guides on when and how to use certain techniques, how to do them, and tips on how to get the most out of them (including tips on how to avoid the mistakes we've made), and suggestions for variations on the basics. We also offer theory—our understanding of why these tools are effective. Our hope is that the theory will make you even smarter about the use of these methods and better able to use them.

If you're an **experienced moderator**, we suggest that the theory will be particularly useful to you too—to think through the "why, when, and how" of using these different tools and techniques. And, having all of these tools between the covers of one book will be helpful to all seasoned moderators in planning projects for both repeat and new clients. We've even found ourselves flipping through these pages as we design our current studies in order to consider all of the options, rather than simply the ones we're personally most comfortable using.

And if you are a **client or an end user of qualitative research**, this book should make you wiser about the research that you are buying, more confident about which tools are good for what issues, and ways to get the most out of each. Beyond this—it's our aim to have everyone thinking in new ways about the potential of qualitative research.

So just to be clear, this is **not** a book about basic interviewing techniques and styles. Don't get us wrong, the basics are critical—absolutely the foundation for what we're about in this book. A moderator needs to know how to introduce a group, lay the ground rules for participation, help people feel comfortable, encourage honest-what's-true-for-them responses, ask questions in non-leading ways, probe for clarification, probe for depth, segue from one topic to the next, and keep the group on course. While we touch on these aspects of interviewing throughout our discussion of various alternative techniques, this is not our primary focus. There are other great books for this material, from old stand-bys (e.g. Goldman and McDonald, 1987; Greenbaum, 1988) to newer publications (e.g. Langer, 2001; Mariampolski, 2001).

THE BIG PICTURE—WHY WE SHOULD CONSIDER ALTERNATIVE TECHNIQUES

As qualitative researchers, we are the conduit between client company and consumer, between service provider and customer. We elicit input from participants, and we relay this to our clients.

What kinds of input are we after? What are we seeking from our client's customers or targets? That varies, of course, depending on the purpose of the project at hand. Part of what makes qualitative research so exciting is the range of subjects explored. Among the topics that we're asked to investigate are:

- What lifestyles people lead—how people spend their time, what they care about, what their life goals are, who and what is important in their lives, what makes them happy, and what worries them.

- What they buy and why they buy.

- How they interact with products and service providers—and especially with our clients' products and services.

- How they feel—about brands, products, categories, the context in which products are used, and the context in which they are purchased.

- What images they hold of brands and experiences.

Well, can't we just ask them?, you may inquire. *Surely they know these things and can just tell us.* We wish it were so easy! But here's what we're up against:

- Memories are not readily played back, like videotapes or the 8mm movies your dad took of you as a child. Rather, they need to be reconstructed in the moment of telling. Respondents usually need help with their reconstructions.

- Emotions and imagery are key to our relationships with brands (see Travis, 2000; Gobé, 2001; Robinette & Brand, 2001). But emotions and images are right-brained happenings, while language is left-brained. Respondents need help articulating their emotions.

- It is said that much of our decision making—as much as 95 percent—is unconscious (Gordon, 2001). We are not quite sure how anyone measures the unconscious so precisely but the implication here is that decisions involve a lot of non-rational input. It is our job to uncover the other-than-rational and the less-easily-discussed. One way we can do this is to tackle the issue from multiple angles, using a range of tools and techniques and remembering to include some right-brained approaches.

Straight questions and answers invite rational thinking. Ask a direct question, and you will get a logical, well-thought-out response. Use the techniques in this book, and you will tap other places in the brain, critical for decision making.

So that is what this book is about: inviting your respondents to approach issues from multiple perspectives and taking the emotional, image-oriented, multi-sensory views into account.

DO'S AND DON'TS

There is a handful of guidelines for using alternative techniques. They help to shore up that foundation that we talked about earlier—they're what you need to know before you can effectively layer on these tools and techniques.

DO create an environment in which people feel comfortable—because many of these techniques involve a level of playfulness and even risk-taking on the part of respondents. For example, a lot of people are not comfortable with their drawing ability, even when asked for a stick-figure drawing. With a comfortable, accepting, fun environment, even the most self-conscious are usually willing and able to participate.

DO give really really really clear directions. This saves time, makes you look like you know what you are doing, and helps to make respondents feel comfortable because they know what's expected of them.

DO encourage respondents to play. Often they surprise themselves with what they can do once you've encouraged them to work outside their usual boundaries.

DO create an environment in which people feel free to speak their minds, even if they are the only ones in the room who feel a certain way. Honoring individual opinions will go a long way toward creating an accepting environment, and ultimately toward providing "truths" that you and clients need to hear.

DO probe. Typically, the exercises are simply a starting point, and the truly rich data comes in response to the subsequent follow-up questions and probing.

DON'T force any participant into responding. Most respondents will jump in and participate in the activities offered in this book. However, if some of them choose not to or seem unable to do an activity, allow them to pass and provide the opportunity for them to play during the next exercise. This is a matter of good research—if they really feel they can't respond, they really might not have anything to tell you. It is also a matter of ethics. Our industry guidelines clearly state that we must "respect the right of any respondent to refuse to answer specific questions." (QRCA Ethical Standards, 1997)

DON'T use these techniques primarily to razzle-dazzle or entertain your clients. Once again, this is a matter of both good research and good ethics.

DO be sensitive to what you may unleash. You use these tools to "go deeper," asking respondents to share their inner-most feelings. It's your responsibility to value their responses and take seriously what they share. Additionally, while rare and associated with particular kinds of topics (e.g. weight loss among the obese), it is possible that using these tools will stir up memories and feelings that are upsetting to respondents. You need to be prepared to handle these situations in a caring and responsible manner. Ethically, the goal is to leave participants in at least as good a place—mentally and emotionally—as when they entered the room.

ABOUT THIS BOOK

Max—your friendly, quirky guide through the pages of the book—tells us that this introduction has gone on long enough and that it's time to get into the meat of the discussion! So here's a preview.

We start with a chapter on *Exploring Experience*. This is about tools that we use to help respondents remember. It ranges from going to the scene of the experience and watching it first hand, to asking people to do some homework before they step into the interview situation so that the experience is fresh, to using memory triggers that are helpful within the group itself.

Next, we present *Laddering*. Laddering—or "Benefit Analysis"—is both a theory and an approach to qualitative interviewing. It's all about discovering the benefits associated with your product, the emotional connections that can be the key to the positioning of your brand.

Going deeper still, we'll tell you in the next chapter about those tools formerly known as "*Projective Techniques*." We've chosen to call them *Metaphorical Techniques*, and in Chapter 3 we will tell you all about how these tools will help you explore images and emotions in rich, juicy detail.

There are times when it is important to get a variety of perspectives on the table in order to get respondents to view the topic from a different vantage point. This can be particularly true when discussing issue-oriented topics, or topics that are loaded with socially desirable content. That's what Chapter 4, *Different Perspectives*, tackles.

Chapter 5 is for miscellany—kind of like the junk drawer, the one you put stuff in because it just doesn't go anywhere else. Effective immediately, however, we are renaming it *The Treasure Drawer* because we think you'll find lots of goodies there. It includes some thoughts about how to take the introductions portion of a focus group out of the ordinary. We also discuss another passion of ours—creativity sessions—and tell you how we feel about the role of qualitative research in ideation.

We bid you farewell in *A Final Word* with one last "tool" that we hope you find helpful—a chart that lists project objectives along with the alternative techniques that we frequently use to address them.

We think there's a logical order to the chapters in this book, but they do not need to be read in order. Each section can stand alone, so use them in the way that best meets your needs. If it's important to bone up on how to use the "Family of Brands" tool for your next project, go ahead and turn to that page. And then next time you are on that long flight from New York to San Francisco, maybe you can read a couple of chapters in their entirety. Or for that matter, go ahead and take this book on your next vacation and read it from cover to cover. We've always wanted to be somebody's beach read, and Max can keep you company while you bask in the sun!

One more word about what this book is not. It is **not** intended as a qualitative cookbook, to be followed step by step. Rather, we give you theories and ways in which the tools have worked for us. We hope and expect that you will take what we offer here and adapt it to meet your needs. And hey—have fun with these techniques. Play with them and make them your own. Adapt them, expand them, extract elements, combine them with others. By modifying them to suit your needs, you'll be "Moderating to the Max!"

CHAPTER 1

Exploring Experiences

(Or: A funny thing happened on the way to the focus group)

HOW PEOPLE REMEMBER

NEWS FLASH: There *are* **NO** *filing cabinets containing memories in the human brain!*

NEWS FLASH: The b*rain is* **NOT** *like a computer hard drive!*

Have you ever gotten that blank stare from respondents when you asked a question? That deer-in-the-headlights look, say when you asked them about the last time they cooked Rice-A-Roni or purchased athletic socks? You may have expected them to simply go to the file drawer in their mind, the one marked R for Rice-A-Roni or A for athletic socks, and pull out the correct incident, details and all. But it doesn't work like that.

Current theory on memory suggests that when we remember something, what we're really doing is constructing the event all over again. Sure, we have some of the parts that we can use to put the memory together, a little like pieces of a puzzle, so it's not a complete fabrication pulled out of thin air. There are sure to be general concepts upon which to draw (the making dinner concept, the shopping concept, the general idea about the emotions that we experience when serving our families a balanced home cooked meal), and specific images (the rack of socks), smells (the burned rice smell from the time we were serving company), and sounds (the annoying sound of bad rock music piped into the shopping mall). But the idea is that remembering is an active process, even a creative process. We craft the memories anew, deleting certain elements, embellishing others, and distorting still others in the telling.

Remembering . . . Hmmmmm

What can you hope to remember about cousin Suzy's wedding? Or your own wedding, come to think about it, when you reflect on it in years to come? Well, that depends, for example on:

• The emotions you experienced during the event.

• How much attention you paid at the time, and what exactly you were paying attention to.

• Your prior experiences, and, consequently, the filters through which you view the event. Perhaps you disliked cousin Suzy's betrothed; certainly, that would have had you attending to and later remembering different events than someone who thought that the fellow was "a hottie."

• Subsequent experiences that have created new understanding and interpretation, that may have you looking on the event with new filters as the years go by. If you have ever been in a relationship that went south, you can surely relate to how your "constructed" memories have changed through the years.

So what does this mean for researchers who need to hear people tell about their life experiences and their memories? This is pretty important—in fact, critical—because a lot of what we do is ask people about past experiences and the emotions, beliefs, and attitudes that go along with them.

Here are some things to think about:

• **Ask questions.** When asking about events that are particularly recent or incredibly salient, it's probably ok to do some straight Q&A. Ask the fantasy baseball addict about his team, and you'll have no problem having him play back the season in more detail than you could possibly want. Ask the antique car owner about this past weekend's car show, or the avid soccer mom about watching her child's games, and your entire two-hour focus group could be taken up with her thoughts, feelings and perceptions.

- **Give participants a memory assist**. When asking about a less salient event or about one that happened in the past, or about one that frequently occurs but has perhaps become routine, you'll want to give your participants a memory assist.

- **Build in time for people to recreate their experiences.**If people are actively reconstructing their memories in response to our questions (and that's what the psychologists are telling us), they need time to do so, especially for those less salient experiences.

- **Offer stimuli that help people talk about their experiences.** This can involve triggers or reminders that people bring from home, or ones that you offer in the context of an interview or a group. It can involve recreating the appropriate context for respondents—through imagination, props or even taking people into the relevant situation. And this is exactly what many of the tools that are presented in this chapter offer—ways of triggering memories so that people can talk richly and meaningfully about their experiences.

- **Create an environment within the focus group that supports the memory process.** This includes a degree of direction (what memory do you want them to create?), a degree of patience, and certainly encouragement!

This is precisely what this chapter is about—the tools and techniques we use to help people recreate their memories.

HOW PEOPLE EXPERIENCE THEIR WORLDS

We've been talking about the fact that memory is a creative experience—that people construct their past in the remembering of it. Well, guess what? The same is true about having the experience in the first place. As we live our lives, we make sense of our world, we give meaning to the events, we subjectively experience our world from our unique perspectives. We create how we experience events. Our experience is exclusively ours because we bring to our life events a whole bunch of stuff that is uniquely us:

- The way we feel in the situation (grumpy or happy, stressed or laid back);

- Our prejudices, both for and against;

- Prior similar experiences and our perceptions and understanding of those events;

- Cultural elements, such as the language we speak, social norms, values;

- And perhaps even whether we had our coffee that morning, fought with our spouse, or listened to our best friend's gossip about the new girl in the school.

Why should you care about how people experience the world? Well, two reasons. The first reason is that knowing how people have life experiences helps us understand what it is we study as qualitative researchers. We're after the thoughts, emotions, attitudes, opinions, beliefs, and motivations of our respondents. We talk to real people who have relevant experiences with particular products, services, or life events, and we learn what is true for them. Notice those words *"true for them"* because they are used deliberately—what we really study is people's individual and subjective experience of their world.

Social Construction Theory and the Value of Qualitative Research

If you're interested in academic underpinnings, think about this. The theory that we've been discussing of how people create their own realities is called social construction theory, and this theory is at odds with the natural science model of research. In the natural sciences, one assumes that there is an objective truth that one is trying to discover, and that one has certain research measures and controls with which to conduct experiments in order to learn that objective truth.

In contrast, the social construction approach says that truth is subjective, dependent on the eye of the beholder. And from this beholder's eye, it seems that qualitative research, not quantitative, is the ideal method for studying subjective truths. After all, we focus on people's experiences of the world, told from their own perspectives and in their own words. From this perspective, qualitative research no longer looks like the poor stepsister of quantitative research.

This leads us to the second reason we should care about how people experience the world. Since the premise is that people create or construct their own realities, we need to consider the kinds of tools, once again, that will support such construction of meaning by our research participants. Thus we are on the lookout for specific techniques that help people create meaning from their experiences. More about this in subsequent pages, but as a hint of things to come, storytelling seems to be one such sure-fire method.

Sometimes people experience something within the very context of our research. We have them interact with new products, react to advertising and new product ideas, and take them on shopping trips. The trick is to make sure that they are given the opportunity to create their own understanding and perception of these events. Stay tuned.

Memory and Experience

Life is a creative happening. We create the way in which we perceive and understand life's events, and we create our memories of the events down the road. Notice—these are not two separate events. What we've experienced colors what we remember, and what we remember colors how we experience life.

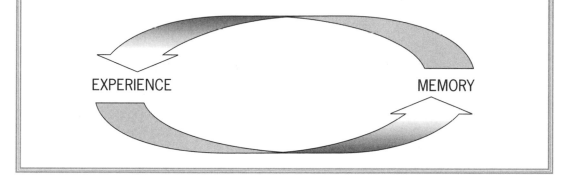

EXPERIENCE   MEMORY

OVERVIEW OF TOOLS FOR EXPLORING EXPERIENCES

So onto the tools already! This chapter focuses on ways to help people get in touch with their thoughts and feelings. Three categories of tools are offered here:

- **Reminder or trigger tools**

  These help people talk more easily and readily about their experiences within the context of the focus group.

- **Pre-Work (aka "Homework")**

- **Free Association**

- **Visualization**

- **Sorts**

- **Storytelling Tools**

  Storytelling tools lead participants into telling their own stories, stories that are relevant to the topic at hand and stories that will yield rich information above and beyond that which is obtained in question and answer formats.

- **On-Site Interview Tools**

  This technique takes full advantage of real-life environments relevant to the client's product, service, or idea. The physical context itself triggers memories more readily than those recreated in the more artificial environment of the traditional focus group.

PRE-WORK (aka "Homework")
Or: My dog ate it, but I want to come to the group anyway

How can you get the most out of a two-hour group? Well, let the respondents get started ahead of time! Seriously, there are some wonderful benefits derived from asking respondents to spend a little time before the interview or group discussion becoming more aware of their surroundings or reflecting on the topic. They have more time to ponder. They can bring in certain things that will help trigger their memories once in the group. And, they can engage in activities ahead of time that will add depth and dimension to their discussions.

When   Use when it's important to gain an in-depth understanding of a person's life experience—either general life issues or issues related to a specific behavior or experience.

Task   To have respondents bring in reports, reflections, recordings, or visuals from home that will help them talk about the issue at hand. These items can establish a tangible context for point of view and assist in the reconstruction of the experience.

Examples   **Keeping a diary about an experience**
                • Using a prototype product and recording the experience
                • Going to one or more fast food restaurants and recording who was there, what was eaten, what the environment was like, and what reactions were produced
                • Shopping for a car and recording what happened and what was felt during each step

                Bringing in an object
                • A child's favorite item of clothing or toy
                • Something purchased from a department store that triggers a special memory
                • Something that reflects the respondent's life right now
                • All of the open shampoo bottles in the respondent's shower

Capturing reflections on an experience through visuals
- A collage (see Chapter 3 for detailed instructions)
- Storyboards, drawn with stick figures (see page 33)
- A "projective" drawing (see Chapter 3)

Telling a story about the topic at hand (see page 37)

Recording a particular environment through photographs, drawings, or audio recording
- Photographs of the respondent's workspace
- Audiotape of the experience of putting a child to bed
- A hand-drawn picture of what is in the refrigerator

Directions

Directions for the activity or activities should be sent to the facility well in advance of the focus group—preferably a week or so for reflective work, and longer if the assignment involves developing photographs or completing other creative endeavors that might demand more time to execute. Instructions should be extremely clear. Some moderators like to put their instructions in a playful font, and include clip art on the page so that the pre-work looks fun and engaging.

By giving respondents an approximate length or time frame for the work they need to do, they'll have an idea of the level of completeness and detail expected (e.g., a two-page story, an 8½" x 11" collage, a roll of at least 24 pictures).

Debrief

It is important to acknowledge and value respondents' time by using the assigned pre-work in the group discussion, even if your objectives have shifted.

Specific debriefs depend upon the purpose of the study and the type of assignment given.

Hints

When the study is bid, inform the facility that pre-work will be required. Depending on the extent of pre-work, be prepared to pay additional incentives. Make sure respondents know pre-work is required when they're recruited and that it's a critical piece of their participation. Warn them it's the "price of admission" to the group.Over-recruit for each group, and send home those who do not have homework, perhaps paying them only a partial honorarium. This also provides an opportunity to pre-screen the homework to select the widest variety or include the more intriguing pieces.

Variation   Ask respondents to come 15–30 minutes before the group is due to start, and have them complete an assignment before they enter the interview or discussion room.

Free Association Overview

Free association is a good way to learn top-of-mind thoughts and feelings on a given topic. Ask a skier the first thing that comes to mind when he or she thinks of a snowstorm and you might hear "fresh powder," "a perfect day on the slopes," "an open fire and a glass of wine." Ask a moderator the same question and the answer might be "missing my flight," "starting an hour late," "only two out of eight respondents!" (Which means maybe we should all quit our day jobs and become skiers!)

The two techniques of free association that we focus on here, Basic Associations and Mindmapping, are used to learn what is commonly and readily associated with a topic—those issues which are close in and easily accessible. Using free association, the moderator begins the journey of understanding an issue from the respondent's point of view. One can think of these techniques as asking respondents for a quick pencil and paper sketch of an issue. In this way, we begin to explore the meaning of the issue from the participant's viewpoint. Over the course of the group, we add color, dimension, and depth; we focus in on particular elements, adding detail; or we back up to learn what else might be included in the picture. But our very first glimpse of the issue—the "sketch"—allows us to begin defining the issue, learning about:

- *Perspective*—How the "picture" or issue looks from the respondent's point of view.

- *Inclusion*—What belongs in the picture and what does not.

- *Tone or mood*—What emotions or feelings might be associated with the issue (e.g., Is the "picture" sunny or filled with rain clouds?)

- *Language*—What words and phrases are used to talk about the issue.

Given that they are used to gather initial thoughts and feelings, free association techniques are helpful when introducing a topic—often at the beginning of a group. By using these techniques prior to more structured discussion of an issue, the moderator gains a fresh understanding of the respondent's perspective. Additionally, because they involve gathering top of mind responses, free association tends to involve questions that are non-threatening and easy for everyone to answer. Thus, they function both as a way to gain an initial look at the issue and as a good way to warm up a group, making respondents feel comfortable and actively involved.

Free association is often done quickly, energetically, and prior to more in-depth probing. The two free association techniques described here, however, can be used as the basis for a deeper look if the moderator chooses to spend more time probing responses for greater understanding.

BASIC ASSOCIATIONS

What do you think of when I say "blue"? Sky, of course. If I say "hammer"? "Salt"? And don't love and ____ go together like a horse and ____? Some associations are obvious, at least to those growing up within the same culture. But then there are associations that are not so obvious—those that are rooted in an individual's personal experience. As an example, one person might associate oatmeal with Mom's home cooking, warmth, and love, while another might think of gluey, yucky cafeteria food. Playing the game of associations with participants is a quick, familiar, and fun entrée into the respondents'-eye-view of the topic at hand.

When	Use when the purpose is to gather top-of-mind responses about an issue or to gain an initial look at the topic through the respondents' eyes, whether that topic is a broad issue or situation, or a specific brand or product.
Task	To ask respondents to say what comes to mind when they think of **X**.
Supplies	None, or alternatively, pencil and paper, even colored markers and paper.
Directions	Identify your topic in general terms (e.g., "mornings," "breakfast" or "Corn Flakes"). Then ask respondents what comes to mind when they think of that topic or issue.
	Ask the group to call out what comes to mind. This encourages group members to build on each other's responses and may stimulate individuals to go in new and different directions compared with what they may do when working on their own.
	Probe for thoughts, feelings, associations, and pictures in their mind.
Debrief	There are two general ways to debrief. You can gather all the responses without probing, looking for the "landscape" and a sense of the big picture, or you can probe for fuller meaning as responses are given. Whichever you choose, ask respondents what themes they noticed, what

stood out, or what was most important to them with regard to the issue. And then follow up on these in further questioning.

Hints   When probing for additional associations, the moderator may want to take the variety of sensory modalities into account, using language that speaks to the full range of styles. For example, to tap into responses of visually oriented individuals, the moderator might ask *"What do you see?"* or *"What pictures are in your mind?"* For the auditory respondents, the moderator might ask, *"What do you hear?"* or *"What do you say to yourself with regard to this issue?"* And for kinesthetic individuals, the moderator might probe for issues related to touch or movement by asking *"What are you feeling?"*

Note that associations can be based on respondents' actual experiences with the topic, or for those less familiar with a topic, on their general perceptions and images.

Variations   Have respondents write down their first thoughts and impressions, and then have them share their observations with the group. This allows time for personal reflection and the potential for fewer "me-too" responses.

Ask respondents to write down the first three things that come to mind when they think of **X**. Have them share with a partner and report back to the group. This serves as a good ice-breaker activity at the beginning of the discussion.

MINDMAPPING

Mindmapping (Buzan, 1974; Wycoff, 1991) is a way of capturing free associations on paper, but in a non-linear way. It's a liberating technique, inviting associations and still more connections and links as the mindmapper plays with the idea. It's the difference between a simple row of sparklers and Roman candles exploding in the night sky! Mindmapping encourages breadth and depth of associations as chains of thoughts and feelings are charted on paper. It is generally considered to be a whole brain technique, tapping into both rational processes of the left brain and emotional and image-oriented processes of the right brain.

When   Use when the purpose is to gain an initial look at the topic through the respondents' eyes and when more detail is desired than can be gathered from a simple free association. Note that mindmapping is a good technique to use when the issue is personal or complex and you want to give the respondents individual think time.

Task   To record multiple thoughts and feelings on a specified topic.

Supplies   Thin colored markers and plain paper, preferably legal-sized paper and an example of a mindmap from a different category drawn on easel paper. The example should illustrate how one association can branch off in a variety of ways, how color can be used, how the mindmap captures thoughts as well as feelings, how both positives and negatives can emerge, and how symbols or drawings can be used instead of words.

              Background music is recommended.

Directions   Teach respondents how to do a mindmap, using a sample that has been generated ahead of time. Tell them that a mindmap is a type of free association—that it is a way for them to write down as many thoughts, feelings, and associations as they can in a short amount of time.

              Next, in a fairly general manner identify the actual topic

being explored (e.g., ice cream or airline travel) and tell respondents that they'll be doing a mindmap on that topic. Then lead them through the process:

1. Tell respondents to put the specified topic in a circle centered on the paper.

2. Tell them that you are going to give them about three minutes to write down everything that they can think of.

3. Encourage respondents to take each branch as far as they can, with at least a couple of connections built on each main thought.

4. Tell participants to work quickly and to fill their entire paper.

5. After about three minutes, the moderator can offer general prompts (e.g., concerning people, places, things, color, and other sensory queries or feelings).

6. Give a 30 second warning before asking respondents to stop.

7. Ask respondents to circle the branch on their ladder that holds the greatest significance to them.

Debrief   Ask for a volunteer to share the one branch of his or her "map" that stood out for them. Then ask if anyone else in the group has anything similar. Discuss all similar branches. Ask a different respondent to share another branch, and so on. Depending upon project objectives, it may not be necessary to explore all branches.

Variations   Have respondents work in pairs or small groups if the topic is one that may benefit from having respondents build on each other's ideas, or if the group energy is lagging.

Create the demonstration example with the respondents, rather than preparing it ahead of time. Chart the group's ideas in mindmap form on the easel. Point out the tactics used in creating the mindmap, such as building a chain of associations and feelings, going back to a word to generate more thoughts, using multiple colors, or using a symbol or drawing rather than a word when the spirit moves you.

Example   **Project Objective:** To explore visitors' experiences at Disney World.

One Respondent's Mindmap:

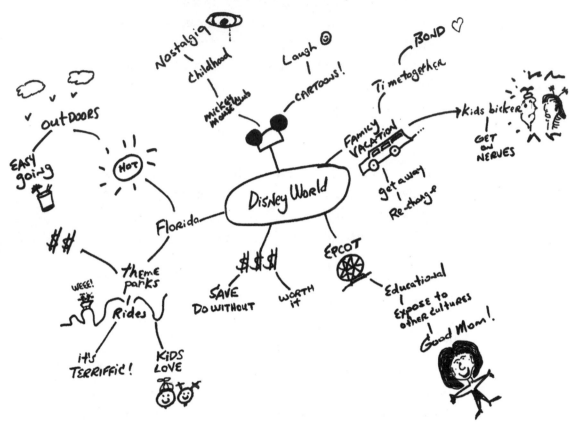

Debrief of upper right branch of the Mindmap: *"Disney World is THE family vacation spot, and family vacations are important to us. We're all so busy working and going to school . . . and then there's all the other activities we've got going on. We need time to get away and just be together—to connect and really feel like a family. And when we get back, the glow usually lasts—for a little while anyway! I guess I'd like to think that being away together makes us closer. But I'm a realist too. Vacations have their bumps in the road. I can usually count on the kids getting into it with each other at least a couple of times while we're away. That's when you want to sell them. But nobody wants to buy!"*

VISUALIZATION

What's in your mind's eye when you hear the word "beach?" Do you see gigantic rolling waves, or do you see little lapping ones? What are you hearing—the call of the gulls or the crash of the waves? Do you feel the sun? Smell the cocoa butter? Presto! You're at the beach. And that's the power of visualization! Conducting a visualization in a focus group is all about bringing into the room some sun and fun—or whatever your topic is—as each respondent remembers and reports the richness of the experience that is uniquely his or hers.

When	Use when it is important to understand respondents' experience in greater detail and richness than they would otherwise be able to give, including what happens and what was felt at the time.
	Visualization can be used to capture a recurring experience, such as cooking pancakes, shaving, or purchasing food from a drive-through restaurant. It can also be used to explore an infrequent but significant event, such as renewing a driver's license, spending time with hospice during a family member's illness, or attending the first day of classes at college.
Task	To take participants through an experience in their imaginations and then ask them to report on it.
Supplies	Paper and writing implement for each respondent.
	Soft, pleasant music is optional.
Directions	• Tell respondents that you are going to take them through a visualization—that you are going to ask them to revisit the experience of **X**.
	• Ask them to get as comfortable as possible, to close their eyes, or to look down if that is more comfortable for them, and to relax.
	• Walk them through the experience, asking questions that allow them to recreate it as fully as possible.
	• Give them time to ruminate and recollect. Take participants through the entire experience before discussing.

- At the end, ask them to spend a minute writing down any piece of the experience that was particularly significant, or that they don't want to forget. Alternatively, give periodic breaks during the visualization to allow them to write down important events.

Debrief

Structure the debrief around the elements of the experience that are most relevant to the purpose of the research. Questions might include:

- *"What was easy?" and "What was hard?"*
- *"How were you feeling in the situation?"*
- *"Who was present?" and "Who was most helpful?"*
- *"What was the best thing about the experience" or "What was the worst thing about the experience?"*
- *"Were there any particular wishes with regard to the service (or product) in question?"*

Hint

Write out detailed instructions for the visualization ahead of time. Consider trying the visualization out on a friend or family member before the project. Read instructions slowly, and pause periodically to allow for reflection.

Example   **Project Objective:** To explore experiences with luggage while traveling on business.

Sample Visualization Script

Setup

"We're going to be talking about business travel—specifically about the suitcase or suit-cases that you take with you on a business trip. Before we get into our discussion, I want you to think about your personal experience with these items—about what it's like to pack up for a trip. I'd like you to start by visualizing this aspect of business travel in as much detail as possible. I'm going to talk you through it, and at the end I'll ask you to stop and write down a few notes to yourself to use in the discussion that follows. Everybody, take a pad of paper and pencil and put it in front of you."

Relax

"So first, get comfortable. Shut your eyes, or if it's more comfortable for you, just look down. Take a deep breath in, and then exhale. Take another deep breath, and exhale. Get any kinks out of your shoulders, your neck. And now one more deep breath."

Visualization

"Picture yourself the night before your business trip. You are getting ready for the trip. Where are you going? What is the purpose of your trip? How long will you be gone? What are you thinking? What do you need to do before you go? How are you feeling?

"Now you are packing for the trip. What is it that you are doing? Picture yourself get-ting your bag. What does it look like? Where do you keep it? You are now choosing your clothes, shoes, personal items. What are you thinking? How do you pack various items—your personal items, shoes, any dressy clothes or suits? Do you have a routine? Do you do anything special?

"Now you are putting your items into your suitcase. What are you thinking? What works well? What is difficult? How are you feeling about the packing process? About the trip overall?

"See yourself at the airport, getting out of your car or the cab. You are walking into the airport. What do you have with you? Anything in addition to the suitcase? How are you carrying things? What is easy? What is hard? How are you feeling at this moment?"

"Think in particular about your suitcase. How do you feel about it? Its look, its feel, its image? What do you like? What don't you like? Will you check your suitcase or carry it on? Picture yourself doing this. How do you feel about it?"

"Now open your eyes and jot down anything that you particularly want to remember. Please write down a couple of wishes that you would have regarding packing up and handling your bags on a business trip."

SORTS OVERVIEW

It's often said that we are defined by the company we keep. Now there's a sobering thought! With whom did you share a grandé soy latte yesterday? Frolic on the beach with in Cancún? Karaoke with at the Fernwood Tap last New Year's Eve?

Efforts to better understand a brand also involve learning about the company it keeps—its frame of reference. What brands does it compete with? What are its strengths and weaknesses relative to that competition? Kind of like who is its karaoke partner, and which one is the lead singer?

That's what sorting techniques are all about—helping to achieve an understanding of how the product, service, brand, or even the company under investigation relates to the competition. Strengths of these techniques include their ability to:

- **Gather** a lot of information on numerous brands quickly.

- **Provide a hands-on activity** that is engaging and often fun. The fact that respondents stand up for most of these exercises can be energizing for the group as a whole (unless they're particularly facile at falling asleep on their feet).

- **Provide stimulus** for discussion and friendly argument.

- **Provide a tangible way** to compare across user or population segments. For example, one could explore how a product is viewed relative to competition among users and non-users of the brand. Or one could ask about the image of a company, exploring across elderly, middle-aged, and young consumer groups.

Of course there are quantitative perceptual mapping techniques. Qualitative techniques are not meant to substitute for these, but rather to offer a starting point for discussion about how products and brands are perceived relative to others in their category.

Many sorting techniques can be used, each meeting slightly different objectives. Those that we'll discuss include:

- *Product sort*—an unaided technique in which participants are asked to sort items into groups that make sense to them. The moderator does not suggest relevant attributes. Rather, these are identified by the consumers in their own language, and explored as participants discuss the result of their sort.

- *Perceptual mapping*—aided techniques, in which the moderator identifies the relevant attributes and items are sorted accordingly. Three types of perceptual mapping are:
  - One Dimensional ("Line-Up")
  - Two Dimensional ("Four Square")
  - Proximity to the goal ("Hitting the Mark," also known as "Bull's Eye")

Although we focus on products, brands, and companies relative to their competition, these techniques could easily be used to explore issue areas. For example, perceptual mapping could be used to explore such issues as perceptions of:

- Different types of service providers, (e.g., local police vs. board of education vs. the local library) in terms of their orientation toward customer service;

- Different types of people on particular dimensions (e.g., different aged people on quality of driving);

- Different political candidates on personal characteristics or their stands on particular issues; or

- How a city or school system compares with an ideal.

PRODUCT SORT

When	Use when the purpose is to identify the relevant competitive set. Additionally, this technique helps to identify which attributes of the product are important and to understand how the target brand or product is similar to or different from competitors on these attributes.
Task	To cluster products, services, brands, or companies into groups that are similar to each other. (Note: The word "brand" will be used in the remainder of this chapter to encompass all of these entities.)
Supplies	Actual packages of products within the category.
	Alternatively, cards can be used—either with only the names of the brands written on them or with both the brand names and logos on the cards.
Directions	Ask all of the respondents to stand and look at the brands on the table.
	Instruct them to place items into groups that have something in common. Different groups should be distinct from each other.
	Tell them that they can form as many or as few groups as they like.
	Tell respondents to work together in forming the groups and to reach a consensus. Reassure them that they will have an opportunity to discuss any differences of opinion that existed among them.
	The moderator may also want to ask participants to organize the groups spatially on the table, placing groups that are most similar to each other closer together and groups that are most different from each other farther apart.
Debrief	Ask respondents to describe the different groups—what makes the brands within each group similar, and how each group is different from the others.
	After the initial sort has been debriefed, ask whether there was disagreement in the sorting process—whether

anyone would have done something differently—and give dissenters an opportunity to voice their opinion. Then ask the group to sort them in a different way, based on a different dimension. Repeat the process as many times as it is productive.

During the debrief, the moderator can also ask if there are any other brands that belong in a group but are missing from the table.

Hints

In giving the initial instructions, the moderator may want to ask respondents to reflect on what is important to them about the brand, or perhaps to think about how they make choices in the category. Suggest that they keep these things in mind as they do their sorting. This tends to focus the respondents on important elements rather than on relatively unimportant but obvious ones, such as the color or size of the package. In fact, if there is an issue or dimension which is not relevant to the purpose of the study, the moderator can explicitly request that the group avoid this when sorting.

It is useful to have a camera available for taking photographs in order to record the results of the sorts for your analysis. Additionally, photos—whether digital or scanned—can be included in reports.

Example

Project Objective: To understand perceptions of the competitive set in the body lotion category.

Debrief of one group's sort: (from left to right)

"Girly Lotions: the ones that have a lot of scent to them; they're sweet smelling or fruity smelling; they're all about fragrance; my husband would never use this (St. Ives and Caress).

Medical: You use these if you have a skin problem, like very dry or itchy skin; I remember using Aveeno soap with the oatmeal when my son had chicken pox, so I bet their lotion would be helpful in the same way (Curel and Aveeno).

Everyday: Lotions that a lot of people use; everyone's tried these; they appeal to lots of people; just good, basic lotions (Nivea and Neutrogena).

Cheapies: when you're on a budget; most of these you can get on sale, or with coupons."

PERCEPTUAL MAPPING

Perceptual mapping (Sabena, 1995) is used to identify a brand's strengths and weaknesses on selected key attributes, relative to the competition.

Line-up: One-Dimensional Continuum

When	Use to focus on one bi-polar attribute.
Task	To place the brand in relation to competitors on a continuum.
Supplies	A roll of paper (e.g., fax or shelf paper), that has been spread down the length of the table. You will have already selected the relevant attribute on which the brands are to be sorted (e.g., value, taste, quality, attractiveness, customer service, indulgence), but you should label opposite ends of the paper with appropriate words indicating the positive and negative poles of that quality (e.g., "Least Valuable"/"Most Valuable"; "Least Tasty"/"Most Tasty"; "Poor Quality"/"Top Quality"; "Most Attractive"/"Least Attractive"; "Best Service"/"Worst Service").
	Have the actual products available, or alternatively, write their names on cards or sticky notes.
Directions	Ask the group to stand and to sort the items on the paper in front of them.
	Tell respondents to place each item where it belongs on the continuum.
	Suggest to the group that they work together, or ask them to guide one person in moving the items into place.
Debrief	Ask respondents to tell about the "map" that they have created, including what was placed highest and lowest and then why they were so placed. Specifically probe to understand how the target brand was placed and how its placement relates to that of the competition.
	Ask respondents where there was controversy, and whether anyone would have placed items differently.

Probe to understand such differences.

Hint   Roll up the paper and take it with you for use in the analysis. Alternatively, a photograph of the "map" will work well to help the analysis, especially when actual products have been used in the sorting process.

Example   **Project Objective:** **To understand what consumers mean when they say some skin care products are more "fun" than others.**

Debrief of Line-up placement, on a scale of "fun":

"Shimmer seems like a product you'd only use when you were going out. It's all about what your skin looks like, not how it is or how it feels. It's not an everyday product, it's just for special occasions.

Sheer is a body lotion, but it's less greasy. Maybe it doesn't work as well as the regular lotion, but the spray bottle makes it seem like it'd be fun and easy to apply.

Firming lotion is a "wish in a bottle." Nothing from a bottle is going to make my thighs firm, so it's not a serious body lotion. But wouldn't it be great if it worked? Maybe. I'd have to try it to see.

Original and Enriched are regular body lotions. Enriched just has a few more vitamins and stuff in it, so maybe it works a little better . . . it's just a little more functional than Original.

Nivea Crème, in a tub, is really serious. It's thick and greasy. It's for curing really dry skin. And Nivea Renewal Night Crème makes me feel like it would have to work miracles overnight. Even the lettering is more rigid and boring compared to the other crème."

Four Square: Two-Dimensional Continuum

When   Use when exploring the interplay between two key attrib-
                utes (e.g., how a women's clothing store is perceived rel-
                ative to the competition in terms of the value and
                stylishness of its fashions).

Task   To place the brand in relation to competitors with regard
                to two dimensions.

Supplies   A sheet for each respondent that shows a simple grid with
                one horizontal and one vertical axis (e.g., high/low value
                and most/least fashionable).

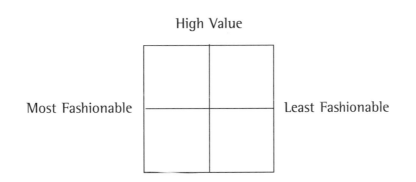

One large grid on an easel sheet, with the same axes as
described above.

Colored dots or colored markers

Directions   Ask participants to place items on their grids according to
                where they belong on each of the two dimensions. Make
                sure respondents understand that they are working with
                two dimensions, and that each is important.

                Once they have completed their individual sheets, ask
                them to transfer the results to the large easel sheet for
                everyone to see, using colored dots or letters to represent
                different brands.

Debrief   Same as with the one-dimensional continuum, previ-
                ously described.

Hint   This activity is more complex than the one-dimensional
              map. Thus, it helps to offer respondents an example from
              a different category. Additionally, this exercise tends to be
              easier for respondents if they have done a one-dimen-
              sional map prior to working with two dimensions.

Example   **Project Objective: To understand the competitive
              arena of soups in order to determine if there is an
              unmet need for a new line of soup products.**

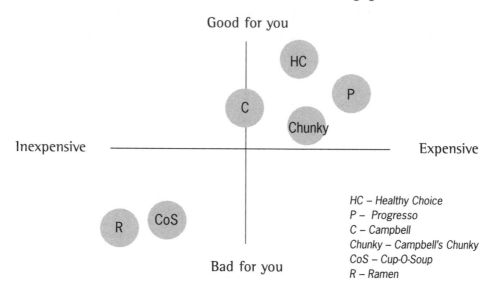

HC – Healthy Choice
P – Progresso
C – Campbell
Chunky – Campbell's Chunky
CoS – Cup-O-Soup
R – Ramen

Debrief of placement on Four Square diagram:

*"Ramen and Cup-O-Soup are instant . . . all the nutrition has
been taken out of them. They're really cheap, good for filling up
my high school boys.*

*Healthy Choice is made to be healthier, it's in the name! Camp-
bell's is the old tried-and-true, right in the middle, and some of
the varieties are probably a little better-than-average for you.
Chunky seems a little more processed, with a few more additives
and thickening agents in it, so not quite as good for you. Progresso has the most natural ingredients, so it seems healthy but
it's also the most expensive."*

Hitting the Mark: Proximity to the Goal

When	Use when comparing a brand to a single goal or ideal. This technique is especially good for measuring the performance of a new product or prototype.
Task	To place several products or brands in relationship to an "ideal," "favorite," or "best." While the moderator asks the participants to focus on an "ideal" or other positive concept, the actual elements that go into making something "ideal" should not be defined by the moderator, but rather self-defined by each respondent.
Supplies	Individual sheets for respondents on which are pictured concentric circles, like a target
	One large target posted on an easel
	Colored dots or colored markers.
Directions	Pass out individual targets to the respondents. Tell them that the center of the target—the bull's-eye—represents the ideal (e.g., the ideal deodorant).

Ask them to place appropriate letters (e.g., P = prototype, S = Secret, etc.) or colored dots (red = prototype, blue = Secret, etc.) onto the target, showing how close they think various products are to the ideal.

Instruct participants to post their individual responses on the large target, so that the entire group can see everyone's placement. All marks for a particular brand should be in a row—on the same radius—in order to facilitate the analysis.

Debrief	Ask participants to tell about their placement of products or brands relative to the ideal and relative to each other—how close the products are to "hitting the mark." Explore individual differences and similarities within the group.

Additionally, probe to understand what elements contribute to something being "ideal."

Example   **Project Objective:** To understand how a new deodorant prototype compares to consumers' "gold standard" (identified by respondents in their group as Secret) for deodorant, as well as how it compares with some competitive brands.

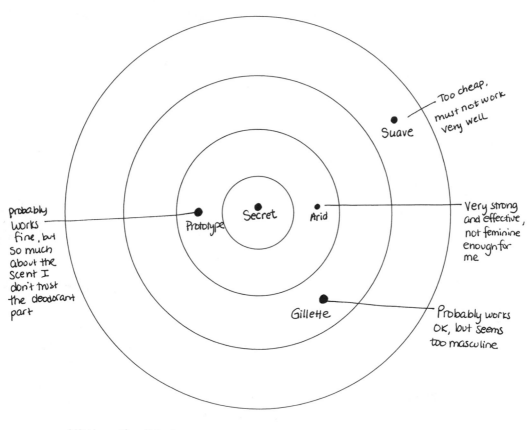

Hitting the Mark

STORYTELLING

"We're all storytellers. We all live in a network of stories. There isn't a stronger connection between people than storytelling." (Smith, 1988)

What Is Storytelling?

When you hear the word "storytelling," what comes to mind? You might remember sitting around a campfire listening to the camp counselor tell scary stories while the wind rustles the trees and every forest noise seems like the wolf man sneaking up behind you in search of a midnight nibble! Or maybe you conjure up the down-home, white bearded man in his rocking chair, corncob pipe between his teeth, spinning yarns. Or if you're lucky, you think of your own father or grandfather recounting tales from his youth.

Now think of your everyday interactions with friends, family and co-workers. Remember the last time you shared some gossip? Illustrated a point with a story from your past? Tried to elicit a "story" from your child about her day? We often share the events of our lives by telling stories. And in doing so, we reconstruct and make sense of our experience, and invite our listeners to learn about and understand it.

> A story is the telling of an event—something happens, over time, in a setting, with characters who are caught up in the plot.

"Storytelling" in the arena of qualitative research is just that—participants recounting the events of their lives—complete with context, plot, characters, detail and texture. Minus the campfire!

Why Storytelling?

Inviting respondents to tell their stories seems like a natural for the qualitative researcher, although it may be just coming into its own in consumer research. Think about it. People live their lives as stories. People talk about their lives through stories. And inviting people to tell their stories in the course of research allows them to recreate and share that juicy experience that we and our clients want to understand.

- Through the telling of a story, the storyteller puts the pieces together, reconstructing the event. Talking about one element of the story often triggers memories for other elements, and the story unfolds.

- Telling a story takes some time, and time allows for the reconstruction.

- A story honors the storyteller's personal and subjective experience—and that's what we're all about, understanding what's true for our participants.

Let's look more closely at why qualitative research and story seem to fit together, like hand in glove.

We live our lives as story. Our own lives are a kind of narrative experience. We live life:

- Over time
- With ourselves, and our friends, family, co-workers and others as the characters in our stories (some bigger "characters" than others to be sure)
- Doing, acting, behaving—as plots thicken and thin
- In settings, from ordinary to extraordinary

It kind of makes you wonder why we don't all bound out of bed in the morning, ready to discover the next chapter in our lives!

We know ourselves through story. We make sense of our experience by telling ourselves and others (what are friends for?) the story of it. We construct and reconstruct those experiences, taking into account the past, our perceptions of the present, and our hopes and dreams for the future. And we discover ourselves in the process.

The story we tell ourselves about who we are is our identity. "Telling oneself about oneself is like making up a story about who and what we are, what's happened, and why we're doing what we're doing . . . self-making is a narrative art." (Bruner, 2001)

We inform others about ourselves through the stories we tell. Storytelling is a natural form of expression. Our everyday conversations are filled with stories. And our respondents try to do the same, although we often cut them off with requests for the headline version.

Tales of Our Lives

Have you heard the one about . . . getting a raise; getting fired; the computer crashing in the middle of working on a (now lost forever) masterpiece; the dog eating my homework; and of course the latest in the sad saga of a waning relationship, . . . it's all fodder for "Tales of our Lives!"

We are more expressive through our stories. The story form encourages the kind of articulation that we, as researchers, hunger for. Through a narrative account, we get:

- Context **and** detail, fact **and** emotion.
- The storyteller's own voice—her choice of words, her emotional tone, what is important to her—and therefore included, and what is not important to her, and therefore left out.

We learn through story. Just like telling stories is part and parcel of our lives, learning from stories is integral to the human experience. We learn about religion and spirituality, other cultures and times past through story. We learn about our country, our community, and the organizations we work in through stories told to us personally or encountered in the media. Stories are a marvelous communicator; when we hear a story:

- We pay attention.
- We are moved.
- We remember.

This is, after all, what Homer knew centuries ago! Similarly, in our quest for knowledge as qualitative researchers, learning through story may help us and our clients to achieve and to remember the insights we seek.

Obstacles to Using Story

So, if narrative is that great, why don't we use it all the time? First of all, lots of studies simply don't call for story. If what we want, for example, is reactions to new product concepts, the research participants don't have experiences around which to tell stories.

Secondly, storytelling does take time and the study design must accommodate the creation and the telling of the stories.

Additionally, the analysis of stories can seem a bit daunting. Stories can provide such rich and abundant information, that it can feel a bit overwhelming to analyze. Stay tuned—we'll offer up some tips for analysis before this tale is done.

When to Use

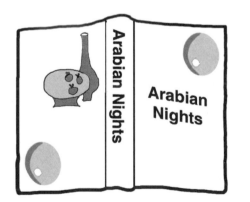

There are lots of times when asking participants to tell their stories will work well to meet the research objectives. Anytime that you want to hear how consumers do, live, act, think or feel in their lives is a good time for a story.

On the other hand, when you want reactions to concepts, prototypes or advertising— then it's probably NOT story time.

Examples of times that storytelling might be just what the client—or Scheherazade's husband—ordered are (Bystedt and Fraley, 2000):

- To **explore a general theme or concept** such as beauty, organization, parent-child interaction, entertainment, or vacation.

- To **explore something that happens over time,** such as:

  A decision process (e.g., the purchase of a car or the choice of colleges).

A period of time (e.g., dinnertime, or the time when your child was seriously ill).

A ritual or routine (e.g., doing laundry, or the family's birthday ritual).

- To **understand a comparison,** for example,

   Before and after—before and after a diet, before and after a new product was introduced, before baby and after baby.

   Then and now—dinner when the children lived at home vs. in the "empty nest" dinner.

   Real and ideal—the way it is vs. the way I want it to be.

   You and me—the way my husband relaxes vs. the way I relax.

- When you want the "**whole story,**" complete with an understanding of the issues and action over time, who is involved, what the context is like, and what feelings are involved.

STORY TOOLS OVERVIEW

Storytelling can take many forms. Consider, for a moment, all of the ways in which you have encountered stories in your lifetime, or in the past week for that matter. For example, stories have been told through the ages as oral history, in epic novels, short stories and poems, through film and photographs, paintings, dance, and more. A variety of story formats work within the research context as well. We can ask respondents to simply tell their stories, or to write and illustrate them, to record a diary, to enact a role-play, or to create a collage or other pictorial representation that tells a story. The form that story can take is limited only by your imagination and the creativity of your respondents.

Task	Ask respondents to tell a story about the topic at hand.
Supplies	Supplies depend on the format called for by the study design. Supplies can include:
	Paper and pen, for writing the story.
	Supplies to illustrate the story, such as magazine pictures, stickers, colored markers or colored pencils, photos taken to illustrate the "characters" in the story or the story setting, or clip art for those using a computer at home.
	Storyboard templates, if asking participants to fill in a storyboard.
Directions	Ask respondents to tell a story about a given theme, event, or issue.
	Reassure respondents that this is something that they can do. For example:

- Specify a story length, such as "at least a paragraph, but not more than two pages."
- Specify the amount of time that they should take to create the story. If the story is being created as homework, the instructions might say—*"take 10–15 minutes to write a story;"* if the story is being created in the focus group, the instruction might be to *"take about 3*

minutes to come up with the outline of your story."
- Note that illustrations can be stick-figure quality, or cut from magazines.

Specify elements that you particularly want respondents to include in the story, given the objective of the research. Story elements might include:
- Who was involved
- Where the story took place
- What happened
- Thoughts and feelings of the central characters
  Be clear that you want a specific story about a specific incident, rather than a description of a general situation. A story with its characters and plot is more likely to provide interesting and insightful detail and emotion.

Deliver the instructions in a fun way that involves participants. For example:
- If instructions are sent to the respondent prior to the interview or focus group, deliver them in friendly and personal language, with a fun type font, and clip art illustrating one or two key points.
- If instructions are given in the group, consider writing them in different colors on the easel, or producing a hand-out that looks fun and inviting.

Tips for probes

As with any interview, you may want to ask participants for more detail about their stories. Some probes to consider are:
- *"What inspired you to tell this particular story, of all those you might have told?"*
- *"What if your child (or spouse or dog or doctor) had told this story? What might have been different? What would have remained the same?"*
- *"What's just outside the 'frame' of this story (i.e. what happened just before or after)?"*

- *"At what point in the story were your emotions at their highest and at what point were your emotions at their lowest?"*
- *"How does the way you felt in this story relate to . . ."* (another situation or incident that the participant has mentioned)?
- *"Tell some more about . . ."* a specific story element that is of interest, such as your feelings in this situation, the setting, who was involved, what happened when you were . . ., the conflict mentioned—what disagreements existed; how were they resolved, if at all; what, if anything, might have made the situation easier.
- *"What does this story say about the product, the brand, your wishes in this category, or your stage of life . . . ?"*

Debrief   After someone tells his story, you can follow up by asking the group whether anyone:

- Has ever had a similar experience?
- Can relate to anything the storyteller has said?
- Has ever had an opposite or very different experience?

Alternatively, you can follow up with the group after everyone tells a story, by asking:

"Thinking about what everyone has said, what are some things that are important in this kind of situation?"

"What are the themes that we've heard in these stories?"

STORY GIVEN AS HOMEWORK: Story with illustrations

Directions   Prepare written instructions with a cover note from the moderator. Ask the facility to send the instructions to respondents at least one week prior to the interview or group discussion. Following is a sample of instructions:

"Please tell a story about:" [The following list illustrates the types of stories that we might ask a respondent to tell. Of course, in any project, only one story idea would be presented.]

• a really terrible clean-up experience

• a typical cleaning experience

• something that happened in caring for your elderly parent

• the birth of your first child

• a visit to your oncologist

• a visit to your grocery store

• shopping for the washing machine that you recently purchased

• a really fun time when you ate ice cream

• feeding your pet

• talking to your teenager about sex

"Include as much detail as you can about the setting, who was involved, what happened, and how you were feeling at the time." [Note that instructions might also specifically ask about product use, depending on the topic of the study.]

"Your 'story' should be at least a paragraph but no more than 1–2 pages."

"Please illustrate your story with pictures. These pictures can be cut from magazines, or can be drawings of your own—stick figures are wonderful and much appreciated!!! Or you can use photos that you have taken. Have some fun with this activity— here's a chance to exercise your creative spirit!"

"Note that I will want to keep your stories, so please use only illustrations that I can keep."

Hints   Consider asking for the story on 8 ½ x 11″ or other
             sized paper that can be easily scanned, so that a sample
             of the stories can be presented in a final report.

             Consider offering a prize to the person in each group or
             across all of the interviews with the most complete story.
             This helps with compliance—but be forewarned, you may
             need to provide a prize to all of the respondents.

Example **Project Objective: To explore issues regarding orga-
             nization in people's lives, including what they find
             difficult to keep organized, and their feelings and
             wishes concerning organization. Information will
             be used as input into ideation for new products.**

             One Respondent's Story (written and illustrated as pre-work):

My Disorganization Story

A long time ago (really, it was a long time ago!), I met this wonderful, handsome, smart, kind man. I fell immediately in love. One of
the things that impressed me so much was how together his
apartment was. I was a mere college student, and he was older,
and unlike me, he had real furniture. His apartment looked, well,
real. Grown-up. He had several antique pieces that he'd refinished,
and it was always tidy. Everything was in its place. And he was
always fixing things—both at his apartment and at my shabby little apartment. I was impressed.

    Fast forward nearly 30 years. (Told you it was a long time.)

Same wonderful man. But 30 years of
accumulated stuff. In fact, while his mother
has often teased him about how neat and
tidy he was, I've wondered where that orga-
nized young man had gone.

    Turns out this terrific man is a pack
rat. He never throws anything out. Our basement is a testament to it. We have lumber
stacked along one wall from all of the projects he's ever done. There are scraps of rug
leftover from a carpet we installed in our first

house (oh this is embarrassing) nearly 25 years ago. Boxes of extension cords, tools galore. Tiles from a house in a different state that we refurbished 15 years ago. "Never know when we might need it!" Heating ducts. A dryer that we replaced seven years ago. Old shower curtains. "They could come in handy." One time I did secretly throw something out—how could he have known? There must have been three or four times that he "needed" it.

When I walk into the basement, I just want to cry. I can't get through the piles and heaven forbid that I actually want to put something of my own down there. How can we begin to sort through all this stuff? For that matter, how can I convince him that he doesn't need it all? I'm really feeling overwhelmed.

We're beginning to think about moving to a smaller house now that the kids are grown, but that would mean a smaller basement. Unless something changes, that just ain't gonna work! What I really wish is that we could sort through all of this and keep only the REALLY essential stuff. Or maybe I could just clean it out when he's on his next (really long!) business trip. He wouldn't divorce me after 30 years, would he?

PHOTO STORY

Directions

This example begins with photographs, and asks respondents to tell a story based on the photographs.

Prepare written instructions with a cover note from the moderator, and ask the facility to send the assignment to participants at least one week prior to the interview or group discussion.

Mail a disposable camera to respondents, or ask them to pick one up from the facility. Alternatively, you can ask respondents to purchase one from their local drug store. Tell participants that you will reimburse them for these expenses. Hint: offer them a flat fee for the purchase of the camera and/or film development—a fee that is generous but reasonable.

Following is a sample of instructions:

"Please use the enclosed camera to take pictures that tell the story of . . . " [A range of examples follow; respondents would be asked to do only one of the following, depending on the objective of the study]
- a typical morning
- putting your children to bed
- a day in the life of your pet
- a typical dinnertime, from the time that you begin to fix dinner to just after everything is cleaned up
- shopping for groceries
- a typical workday

"Take the entire roll of film, illustrating in as much detail as possible what this experience is like for you, then have the roll developed."

"Tape the pictures onto standard-sized paper [8 1/2 x 11"], and write a caption for each."

"This is a chance to exercise your creativity!! Have some fun with this. You may want to involve your child [or spouse or co-workers] in the project."

Hint   Respondents may need permission to take photographs in some locations. For example, if asking for pictures from work or in the grocery store, they will probably need the cooperation of management in each location.

STORY CREATED DURING THE GROUP DISCUSSION OR INTERVIEW

Memory Triggers

Directions   During a focus group, ask participants to tell a brief story about a specific aspect of the study's topic.

Pass a hat (or other fun container) and ask each respondent to take a slip of paper. On the paper is written an element of the topic at hand. Or, provide a list of elements that you are interested in, written on the easel, and allow respondents to choose.

Ask the participants to tell a "short story" about their topic, including specific items such as what happened, who was there, where they were, what was said, and how they felt.

Example   *Leisure Hotel Stays*

Each participant would base a story on one of the following story elements:

- A typical breakfast at the complimentary buffet

- Taking children to the hotel

- Worst experience

- Best experience

- A time when you were impressed by your hotel stay

- A recent memorable stay

- Staying in a suite hotel room overnight

- Staying in a conventional hotel room overnight

Hints   Give respondents a few minutes to prepare. Note, however, that 3–5 minutes will usually be adequate. One professional storyteller claims it is his experience and that of others in storytelling workshops that the pressure of producing a story in a short amount of time forces amazingly detailed memories and coherent stories.

Create a safe environment before asking respondents to tell stories with minimal preparation. Suggest that they have fun with the exercise, and let them know that whatever they are able to tell will be useful and important.

STORYBOARD

When
Use when there is a need to understand a sequence of events.

Directions
Hand out a storyboard template, and ask participants to fill in the stages or steps involved in the topic at hand.

Ask respondents to fill in details that you might want to know at each stage, such as:

- How they felt

- Who was involved

- Any products used

Debrief
Ask one respondent to describe her steps in the process.

Ask others if they have anything similar.

Ask for differences.

Ask, based on everything they've heard, what are the most important steps in the process.

Hints
Make your template look fun—on colored paper or with colored text and pictures.

Probe for emotions if you want them—the sequential nature of the exercise will be likely to encourage rational and linear thinking.

Example
Project Objective: To understand the relationship between pet owners and their pets.

A DAY IN THE LIFE OF YOUR DOG: Please write the story of a typical day in the life of your dog, in as much detail as possible. Include both your thoughts and feelings, and what you imagine those of your dog to be. Underneath each, please add a drawing or a symbol that goes with each step in your dog's day. Use as many pages as you need to.

Pix of Dog

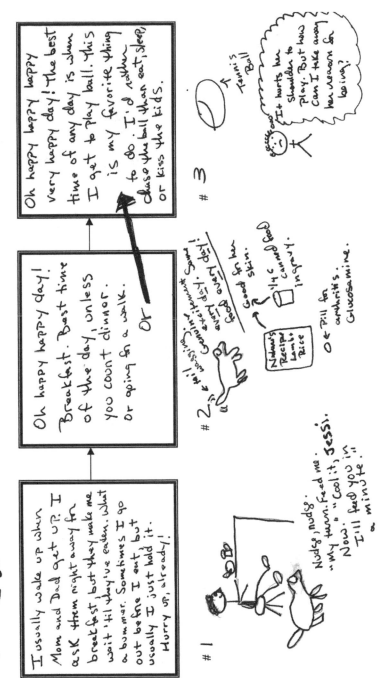

More Variations on Storytelling Techniques

- Ask respondents to bring a relevant **photograph** to the group (e.g., a photo that "captures your child in her favorite outfit;" a photo from a birthday party; a photo taken during a typical evening meal). Have them tell a story based on the photo.

- Prior to writing a story, ask respondents to **relax** completely and let their minds wander. Once they are completely relaxed, ask them to ruminate, dream, or allow their thoughts to muse over the subject matter at hand. After 5–10 minutes, ask them to jot down the images, thoughts and feelings that they had, and to construct their story using something that occurred to them during the relaxation process. [See instructions on visualization, for tips on how to help people relax. Note: This could be done as part of a homework assignment, or, with a shorter timeframe, in the context of a focus group].

- **Thinking backward:** ask participants to *think* about a particular topic in their present lives, and to track that topic backwards in time. For example, if exploring the significance of cars in people's lives, the respondent might be asked to start with their current car and to recall significant memories associated with cars, back to the earliest time that they could remember.

  Alternatively, ask participants to track a *feeling* state backwards in time, such as romantic love or intimacy associated with family vacations.

- Ask participants to start the storytelling process with some sort of timeline. They might be asked to create a timeline that reflects big picture events, e.g.:

  "Place three life changing events on a timeline,"

  or to construct the timeline with more mundane (yet important to clients trying to understand their brand!) events pertaining to their use of a product or service, e.g.,

  "Create a timeline that represents the significant events in your coffee drinking experience."

The story would be based on one or more of the events on the timeline.

- **Watching for a story:** ask participants to watch what happens over a period of time with regard to the subject at hand. They might take notes or journal about their observations. Ask them to write their story at the end of the time period. For example, over the period of a week, participants could pay attention to what happens during the dinner clean-up, or with regard to interactions around their children's homework, or in their efforts to lose weight. Their story will reflect what they have observed during that time period.

Analysis Tips for Stories

There are many possible ways to analyze and report findings based on stories. Consider these as ways to utilize story findings:

Identify themes across participant stories:

- Relying in part on the themes and ideas that participants themselves perceive as important
- Relying in part on knowledge of the category and the client objectives.
- Being open to insightful ideas frequently mentioned by participants.

Look for specific elements across stories, depending on the objectives of the study, e.g.:

- Track the steps in a decision process.
- Examine the use of a product, and the context in which it is used.
- Look for a precipitating event of some kind—for example, what inspired use of a particular product or service?
- Explore emotionality across stories, and its apparent causes.

    Search for a unifying myth or archetype that organizes the data or appears to underlie consumer feelings about a product or a brand.

    Let the stories speak for themselves, much like Studs

Terkel does in his book *Working*. This may be useful when having interviewed a small number of people, carefully chosen for particular expertise or other remarkable attributes. It may also be useful as a preliminary data gathering effort, prior to a larger study.

ON-SITE INTERVIEWS
Or: Taking the show on the road

Who says qualitative research has to be conducted in front of a one-way mirror, around a conference table, with M&M's in the back room?

What if, instead of having respondents bring something to the group as a trigger for their memory, we have them go to the source? What if we see respondents in their own worlds? Think about all the triggers and cues that would be available to help them recreate an experience, recall a feeling, or explain themselves to us in a rich and meaningful way. Wow!

Going on-site to learn about behaviors, attitudes, perceptions, and experiences is nothing new. Margaret Mead saw the value in living with Samoan Islanders to try to understand their personalities and practices. Heck, Jane Goodall lived with gorillas! Anthropologists have long studied different cultures by observing people's behaviors first-hand over a set period of time.

What to Call Them?

Ethnographies? This term is usually associated with anthropologists who spend long periods of time living with and sharing the lives of people in a particular culture, patiently watching what happens, then drawing conclusions based on their observations. But this doesn't really fit what we do as qualitative researchers. We do more than just observe. We prompt and probe, question and clarify, and discuss what's going on with respondents in an attempt to further our learning.

In-Home Interviews? But our interviews aren't limited to homes or apartments. We can go anywhere that provides the context we want to explore, whether it's an office, a job-site, a beach, a restaurant, a teenager's room, or a used car lot.

On-Site Interviews? This feels pretty close. It's definitely about being on-site—whatever the site—with respondents. So that's the term we'll use in this chapter.

When to Use

As we've already discussed, typical focus groups and depth inter-views rely on a respondent's ability to recall events, behaviors, or impressions and then relate them to the moderator with as much accu-racy as the respondent chooses or is able to impart. On-site interviews allow the moderator to get one step closer to actuality. And they can be an excellent way for moderators to meet their qualitative objectives, especially when there is a need to:

- **To understand the big picture of the target's life in order to eventually see how a product or category fits in.**
  Often clients engaging in new product development, considering an acquisition, or working in a new category may wish to explore who the target is or how people use or interact with particular products.

- **Learn more about what drives people.**
  Who are they? What makes them tick? What shapes their deci-sions? How do they arrange their milieu, be it their in-home or at-work surroundings?

- **Understand behavioral nuances about product usage.**
  Subtle behaviors aren't always easy to report in a focus group discussion, but they can more readily be observed, questioned, and detailed by watching someone actually use a product or ser-vice.

- **Explore misperceptions or gain clarification of reported be-haviors.**
  When certain reactions and behaviors don't necessarily make sense, on-site interviews can help immensely. For example, you may find consumers are using a brand name as a generic—they'll say "Kleenex" instead of "tissue" in the focus group room (which could be especially telling if your client is Puffs!). On-sites give you a chance to see for yourself what's in their tissue box.

- **Identify unmet needs.**

  Clients considering new product development can explore current behaviors and practices and use the learning as a starting point for idea generation sessions (see Chapter 5) or concept development. And further along in the product development cycle, they can observe prototypes being used in real life settings.

- **Understand the general context of people, products, and ideas.**

  All of these objectives can benefit by interviewing respondents within their own worlds, getting closer to their experiences, using their artifacts and surroundings as starting points for discussion and as cues for helping them remember. Imagine the difference between asking people how they vacuum, even prompting them to be specific and detailed, compared to watching them pull out, plug in, maneuver, struggle with, bend over, untangle, curse at, and put away the vacuum. Compare your perception of what teenagers tell you is important to them vs. looking at what's hanging on their walls (Is it a poster of Barbie or Britney? Are there photos of their families or their friends?)

And don't forget, the unexpected can often lead to gems of discovery. When the kids come home during an on-site interview about snack foods, they can get involved in the discussion and share their opinions as well. Having nearby relatives or neighbors drop by provides insights about the built-in support new moms have cultivated. Sitting in someone's office can give you a sense of how busy that person is or the level of distraction, based just on the phone calls or drop-ins that occur. Given the opportunity, respondents will show you the unique ways in which they use a product. And who could ask for anything better than a spilled bowl of cereal and a crying child to get a richer understanding of cleaning rituals or of those products a homeowner has available for clean up?

Some Sample Probes

Use the on-site environment to its fullest advantage

- *"Show me something that represents who you are or what's important to you."*
- *"What is something you're proud of?"*
- *"Tell me the story about this picture and why it's one you've displayed."*
- *"Where in the house are you most relaxed? Take us there and show us what makes that area especially relaxing for you."*
- *"You said that you are frugal. Can you show us some examples of ways or times that you were frugal?"*

Ways to explore the target's context

- *"Let's go on a hunt around the house for all the different ways you use plastic storage bags."*
- *"How do you organize your pantry? What are the different "clusters" of products you have on hand, and why are they stored where they are? I see canned fruits on one shelf, and applesauce on another—what's your thinking on this?" Or, "What were you thinking when you placed them there?"*
- *"If you purchased an antibacterial soap, where would you keep it? Where would you store it? Let's see with which other products it'd be kept. Why there and not over here?"*
- *"Why are these bottles at the front of the bar shelf, and the others further back? And what's this bottle of Jack Daniels doing on the counter? How do these bottles get placed where they are?"*

Ways to explore a behavior or process

- *"Show me where you keep your reference materials. Walk me through how you would find information on particular office supplies you use."*

- *"We'd like to watch as you do a load of laundry. Explain each step you take and how you do it."*
- *"Using the product we've provided, go ahead and fix yourself a snack the way you normally would at this time of day."*
- *"Demonstrate the aspect of vacuuming you hate the most. Tell us each new thought and feeling you have as you go through this process."*
- *"Go ahead and order pizza the way you usually would for home delivery. Let us hear your side of the phone conversation, and then we'll talk about what was happening on the other end."*

Ways to explore language or behavior inconsistencies

- *"Hmmmm. You said you keep all your cleaning supplies in the pantry, and I see your mop and broom here, but you got the vacuum out of the family room closet. Is that where you typically keep it? What's the difference?"*
- *"You keep calling this 'Pine-Sol,' but I see that the label says 'Mr. Clean.' What is this product? What do you call it in your own head? How did you come to call it that?"*
- *"You've said you buy only generic toilet paper. Yet I see Charmin in this closet. Can you explain this?"*

Things to Keep in Mind with On-sites

Of course, a moderator must be extremely flexible and adaptable during on-site interviews, probably even more so than in a focus group. (Think Silly Putty! Think rubber band!) You are not only the interviewer, but also the planner, the director, the coordinator, the host, and the one who's going to make it all happen seamlessly within the allotted time.

So, some considerations . . .

By inserting yourself into someone's life, you really are a guest for the period of the interview. The beauty of being on-site is being able to observe reality. What that means is the businessman can't ignore an urgent request from a client or boss. It means that a toddler may want to chew on your stimuli. And it means a beloved pet will invariably nuzzle the client who is most allergic or most uncomfortable around animals. (Note to self: "Determine any client allergies and work appro-

priate questions into the screener— or else carry antihistamines!") So learn from what you're experiencing. Feel free to question the regularity and importance of what's happening around the respondent since it might very well have an impact on the topic.

If you think clients tend to have unrealistic or heightened impressions of who their customers are, wait until they visit their users in person. It may be necessary to remind clients that, as long as screening was on target, these are the people using their products—regardless of their dress, demeanor, housing, or quirks. On-sites can often broaden a client's perceptions above and beyond what happens in a focus group facility. This is reality. Or at least it offers a closer approximation to reality than being in a facility.

Remember, it takes a lot of energy to travel from interview to interview, balancing the logistics and the objectives, while also lugging all your AV equipment and stimuli. And there is a greater potential for the unexpected to happen. All of these challenges make this methodology physically and mentally challenging, but they also make for a lot of fun.

Setting Up On-sites

The most important consideration when conducting on-sites is treating respondents ethically and with dignity. There should be full disclosure in terms of what the research will cover and how the research will be used. Respondents should not be asked to do or show you anything that pushes them beyond their level of comfort. As the coordinator of the entire event, the moderator should personally take responsibility for not mistreating a respondent or diminishing his trust.

Where to hold them

Of course you'll choose the location for your on-sites depending on the objectives of your study and what environment you want to see. It would be silly, for example, to interview a teacher in her home if everything you're interested in happens in her classroom.

You can conduct an on-site interview just about anywhere a person can be focused enough to answer your questions, and comfortable enough to work with you. You'll also need a location that is practical for the logistics of audiotaping or videotaping or for bringing a client team along. It is kind of hard to bring everything and everyone needed on an airplane in order to talk to a business traveler. Think of the expense! (Then again, think of the frequent flyer miles!) But what about setting up at an airport?

Logistically, the following types of locations can be considered:

- To understand who respondents are and what's important to them, consider locating the interviews in their own environments, such as a teenager's bedroom, a salesperson's office, or a soccer mom's car.

- To observe them using or storing a product, think about going into their kitchens, to job sites, in office supply rooms, behind a bar, at the gym, on the beach.

- To learn about shopping for a product, accompany them to a mall, a grocery store, a fast food restaurant.

- To understand a particular event or experience, consider holding interviews during a community fair, at a resort hotel, or on a train.

Remember to Probe

- Don't forget to probe in order to learn more about respondents' perceptions!

- If respondents claim their cars are their pride and joy, ask them to show their cars to you.

- If they think washing windows is a hassle, ask them to demonstrate exactly what they mean.

- If they believe their printer is the slowest in the world, time it with them.

Something else to consider about locations: Do you need permission from someone other than the respondents in order to conduct the research in your desired location? If the answer is yes, obtaining the necessary authorization in advance from a store or other establishment allows the research to be conducted without interruption.

Client team

A key component of an on-site project is the client team. Always try to have **at least one but no more than three** people from the client team attend an on-site. Here's why:

- Actual observations are far more meaningful than reading reports, watching video clips, or even living through an entire videotape. Being in the moment provides enormous learning opportunities, beyond what might be covered in a guide.

- Using contextual cues can allow new directions of learning.

Debriefing discussions among the team immediately following the interview or set of interviews allow insights and observations to be noted, commented on, and explored. Each observer is likely to have his or her own perception of what happened.

In this scenario, there are several people walking into the on-site, and not one of them is hiding behind a one-way mirror, so each one needs a job.

There are a number of benefits to putting the team to work. Giving them each a job keeps them involved. Second, respondents will be more at ease when they understand that everyone has a purpose, instead of feeling as if they have a gallery of people staring at them or hanging onto their every word. Third, there are so many dimensions of an on-site interview, that asking each team member to focus on something distinct has the potential of uncovering different observations or leading to new questions.

Assignments you can give include:

- *The Eyes:* someone who can work the video camera and who can pay special attention to observing what's going on—who else is in the background, what's on the walls, where products are located, the condition of the environment.

- *The Ears:* someone who pays close attention to exactly what is being said. Ideally, this person will have a notebook and can capture in writing as much of the conversation as humanly possible, as well as mark any quotes of particular interest.

- *The Wild Card:* someone who can manage a still camera and any stimuli you need (and perhaps manage your baggage if you can convince them it's for the sake of the research!).

Importantly, *all* should have paper and pen to jot down key insights as well as any additional questions they might have.

Take Pictures

It's great to have a digital camera to capture stills in addition to videos, because a digital camera allows you to access key pictures immediately. Sometimes just a face is enough to remind you of the interview, a key insight, a major difference, etc. If inclined, you can review photos with the client team that same day or create a quick PowerPoint presentation for any debriefings you conduct. Also, adding photos to your report or presentation can help bring the research to life.

Setting respondent expectations

Some individuals may be concerned about allowing a stranger—or a team of strangers—into their homes. They must be told what to expect as they are recruited, so they know that two or three people (interviewer and viewers) are planning to show up on their doorsteps. Similarly, if video or still pictures will be taken, participants should be forewarned since some people are hesitant about allowing cameras into their home (for security reasons) or workplace (for confidentiality reasons).

Since understanding the environment, situations, and contextual cues, as well as observing behaviors, is such a valuable component of this type of qualitative research, capturing visual reminders via video or pictures is highly recommended. Sometimes budget, timing, availability of equipment, or even the subject matter may not allow for use of video as a means of capturing images, so compromise and improvise. (It takes much longer to view and edit video than it does to actually shoot it. It also costs a pretty penny to have an outside firm edit videos for you.) Digital and 35mm still photos can be an alternative to extensive use of video. Keeping a page of "visual observations" could also work to supplement photos. However, nothing will take the place of video if you want to capture the process of Dad brushing his teeth or Junior playing on the newly installed swing set.

Recruiters should encourage respondents not to do anything different in preparation for the interview, like cleaning or organizing or laying out products or anything else they might think is helpful. It should be impressed upon them that the interview is very much about ordinary life in order to get a glimpse of what their day is like in reality. They are not expected to host a party! Similarly, interviewer and clients should not expect refreshments nor walk in asking to use a restroom. Be professional and be prepared.

Inform respondents prior to the interviews about the level of attention you'll need. You may choose to allow or encourage interruptions, which could add to your learning. Or you might want to specify that you'll need two hours of undivided attention. Whatever you need should be determined by your project objectives and communicated to the respondent ahead of time. In other words, if you want to observe pizza being ordered, delivered, and eaten at home, preparations should be made for the family to be there, and they should plan on eating dinner during the interview. It's hard to understand the family dynamics of mealtime if the kids are at a play-date and Dad is working late.

Dynamics of the Interview

Which leads to the question of who's in charge. Establishing the interview as a one-on-one—meaning only one person asks questions of the respondent—seems to work best. It's easier for respondents to focus on one person's questions rather than dividing their attention among all three. Additionally, the respondents are less likely to feel overwhelmed or "attacked" by the group if there is a primary interviewer. This approach gives you, the professional moderator, the ability to conduct the interview in your own manner, handling all the complexities of the interview—key objectives, flow of the guide, comfort of the respondent, new directions to take—and insuring everything will be covered in the best way possible.

You can and should set aside time during the interview to allow clients to ask their questions—possibly between sections or before changing topics, and definitely at the end of the interview. Each moderator and team will need to find the interaction that works best for them, and this is best agreed upon prior to the start of the interviews. But keep in mind that the comfort of the respondents is most important.

Debriefing with the Client Team

As soon as possible after the interview (perhaps even in the car as you're driving away), it is helpful to have the team work together to complete a summary sheet. This immediate debriefing allows you to hear what the clients took away from the interview as well as to record the salient points for future reference. And, it sure beats trying to review hours and hours of videotapes to put together a top line!

This on-the-spot debriefing can be done with a form that is designed ahead of time, (e.g., a page or two with space for notes under the headings of different sections of the guide). Or a debriefing could simply be an ongoing list of new thoughts and insights. It can be done "group think" style or individually and then shared as a group. No matter how it's done, it's important to capture and share all the different observations, both what was seen and what was heard, in order to build the learning and get as much out of each interview as possible.

Large group debriefs can also be held periodically, bringing together:

- **Different observers**, each of whom may only have seen a few of the interviews. Since there are often many clients interested in experiencing this type of interview, the composition of the client team frequently changes in an effort to maximize the number of individuals experiencing the research.

    A word to the wise here: Insist that each individual see at least three interviews, avoiding the problems that can arise when someone happens into an interview that is an anomaly! Avoid having clients arrive or leave during an interview, because you want this to be a team interview and you want to minimize interruptions and distractions.

- **Different teams**, if more than one research team has been in the field.

A large group debrief insures that everyone is on the same page, consistencies and similarities are identified, and differences are noted or explored.

A Bonus!

A side benefit that often occurs is that the client team bonds during an on-site project. Perhaps it's a bit of "living the challenge" and "coming through it" that forges new bonds. Or maybe it's the evolution of learning that brings them together. But whatever the reason, client teams usually have a better appreciation of each other, as well as a better understanding of their target, after an on-site project. They also have some great new stories to tell back at the office!

Miscellaneous Tips (Or: Do what we say, not what we've done)

On-sites can make you a believer in Murphy's Law: Anything that can go wrong, will go wrong! So being prepared might ward off some of the following possible catastrophes. (Believe it or not, all these suggestions are based on personal experiences, so trust us.)

- Bring **extension cords** for your camera and cassette recorder, so you're not balancing the camera on the back of the couch or having to crawl under someone's bed to access the closest outlet. Also bring plenty of batteries in case there is no power or none that is easily accessible.

- **Videotape** *and* **audiotape if possible.** That gives you back-up. But acoustics are different in every location, so be aware of background noise from AC, fans, TVs, or music that can interfere with the sound quality. And be sure to place the video and audio mikes in slightly different locations, so if one fails, the other might be salvageable.

- Always have **extra video and audio cassettes** in case the interview runs over. You don't want to miss precious comments because your tapes are in the car.

- Unless interaction with children is of interest, consider requesting a **babysitter** or some other childcare arrangement if you'll be interviewing parents. The respondents should know you'll need their attention for most of the interview. In the absence of a sitter, know that your interview time might (will!) be fragmented because attention is likely to be diverted to the kids. Alternatively, carry a box of crayons or a puzzle or games to occupy a child who happens to wake up early from a nap.

- Hire a **driver** who knows the area and can get you from interview to interview regardless of traffic, detours, or last minute changes. This means you won't get stuck parallel parking six blocks from your interview, lugging equipment and stimuli through the rain, and forgetting to put another quarter in the meter halfway through the interview! An added bonus is that the driver can usually suggest good places for a quick bite to eat, where the cleanest restrooms are, and even add some insights about the neighborhood or history of the area that could be useful for gaining more insight into the context of the interview.

- Give the facility your **cell phone number,** and check messages as often as possible. Last-minute cancellations or replacements need to be communicated to you, lest you show up at an interviewee's door only to find no one home, or worse—that the respondent is sicker than a dog!

CHAPTER 2

Exploring Experiences and Decision Making—"Laddering"

(Or: Climbing up to go below the surface)

What is "going below the surface" anyway? We hear clients ask for it. We hear moderators lament about not attaining it. Yet do we really know what it is we're seeking "below the surface?"

Well, ask no more. You've come to the right chapter! Because once you understand laddering, you'll not only know what's below the surface, you'll know how to get there too!

Let's start on the bottom rung . . .

WHAT IS LADDERING— AND WHY SHOULD I CARE?

Laddering is a qualitative methodology that was introduced in the mid 1980s by Thomas Reynolds and Jonathan Gutman, then on the faculty of the University of Texas and the University of New Hampshire, respectively. It's based on Gutman's Means-End Theory (Gutman, 1982), the underlying theme of which is that decision makers (including consumers) choose a course of action (including purchasing goods and services) based upon the likelihood of its achieving important outcomes (Reynolds and Olson, 2001). Those important outcomes are better known to us as benefits, and those benefits are both functional and emotional.

Essentially, laddering is a systematic exploration of the links that exist between basic product/service attributes (physical characteristics, intangible features, facts) and the meanings, feelings and associations they impart (functional and emotional benefits). The basic model of laddering's hierarchical structure, which closely aligns with our own cognitive structure, looks like this:

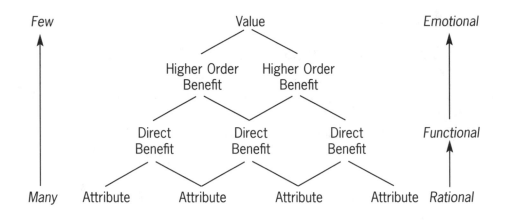

In order to fully understand the model, it'll be helpful to keep in mind several important concepts:

- There are many rational **product/service attributes,** often too many for consumers to remember—or care about!

- Attributes converge in a smaller number of **direct benefits,** functional benefits that are *directly* connected to the product/ service.

- Direct benefits converge in an even smaller number of **higher order, emotional benefits,** emotional benefits that are *indirectly* connected to the product/service.

- Higher order benefits converge in a finite number of **core values,** or human ideals.

- The higher levels are ultimately more motivational than the lower levels. In fact, as Reynolds and Gutman theorize, they drive the decision-making process.

Many of the higher order emotional benefits and values commonly seen on ladders are the same you undoubtedly had lively discussions about in your Psych 101 class—the ones that appear in Maslow's Hierarchy of Needs and Rokeach's Value Inventory:

Rokeach Value Inventory

Commonly Seen on Consumer Ladders	***Not Commonly Seen on Consumer Ladders***
comfortable, prosperous life	inner harmony
pleasure/enjoyable life	spiritual intimacy
stimulating, active life	wisdom
happiness	salvation
freedom/independence	world peace and beauty
equality	
accomplishment	
respect/admiration	
friendship	
health/physical well-being	
sexual intimacy	
security	
self-esteem	

Let's look at an example from the world of consumer goods: laundry detergent. The various levels of the ladder might include:

So in selecting and using laundry detergent, what's really important is the desired outcome or emotional benefit: to look good, be admired by others, and ultimately, feel good about oneself. The attributes of a product—color-stay bleach, for example—are simply a means to that end.

Understanding desirable benefits and how any given product or service achieves them is synonymous with understanding "why," and understanding "why" is synonymous with understanding motivation. BINGO! The marketer's Holy Grail: **Motivation!** That's what is below the surface!

And why is it important to understand motivation? Because leveraging motivation leads to:

- Effective marketing strategies.

- Enticing advertising.

- Successful new products, services, programs, and policies.

While Laddering is commonly described as an interviewing technique, it's a lot more than that. As you may have already gathered, it is a philosophy. But it's not just any philosophy. It is the one that should guide qualitative research whenever the object is to understand "why"—to discover motivation. In the case of marketing products and services, this is commonly sought in the early stages of strategic work when positioning or re-positioning the brand.

That being said, let's move on to the nitty-gritty: How to conduct the interview and analyze the data. Ready for the second rung?

CONDUCTING THE INTERVIEW

The laddering interview is conducted with individuals (one-on-one's) or small groups (triads or mini-groups). We frequently use a combination of the two: one-on-one's to identify the basic structure, small groups to enhance descriptive meaning and situational context. When first learning or practicing laddering, however, use the one-on-one format. It's less complicated and easier to track.

All respondents in the sample must be category users and all relevant competitive brands within the category should be represented. Non-users and rejectors are typically not interviewed in a laddering study simply because the product/service has little meaning in their lives. As such, they do not realize benefits and, therefore, are unable to articulate them. No benefits = no ladders!

Sample size is relatively small, ranging from 15–20 one-on-one's for a straight-forward category such as laundry detergent (or 4 to 6 one-on-ones and 3 to 4 mini-groups) and as many as 50 one-on-ones for a complicated category such as automobiles (or 10 to 15 one-on-ones and 6 to 8 mini-groups). As in any qualitative study, the total number of interviews is also dependent upon segment variables (e.g., regional differences, competitive brand representation). Regardless, larger scale samples are not warranted as there is only a limited number of hierarchical concepts in our cognitive structure and a limited number of end values that we seek—remember Rokeach!

THREE BASIC COMPONENTS OF THE INTERVIEW

The purpose of **the first step** of the interview is to identify relevant attributes (e.g., physical/tangible characteristics, intangible features, facts). This is accomplished by asking the respondent to think about and discuss the product or service in ways that help to identify key distinctions--those that are typically rational. This is most often accomplished via open-ended probing (e.g., *"What do you look for?" "What's important to you in this situation?" "What is it about X that you prefer?" "How would you describe it?"*). Distinctions can also be uncovered via triadic sorting. In this method, three products or services within the same category are exposed. The respondent is then asked to identify one or more ways in which one of the products or services is different from the other two. This same process continues using various triads of competitive products or services until distinctions (attributes) have been exhausted. We've found that open-ended probing works just fine and is generally more efficient than the triadic sort. Try the sort sometime, though. Providing visual stimuli can be helpful to some respondents.

The second step in the interview is to identify which attributes uncovered in step one are most important or operative in the decision process. This is accomplished by asking the respondent to place each attribute into one of the following categories: very important, somewhat important, not important. This prioritization is essential because the respondent can articulate only the benefits derived from attributes that hold personal significance. If an attribute is not important, in other words, little or no benefit will result, rendering the next step of the interview unproductive and meaningless. This bears repeating: No benefit = no ladders!

The third and final step of the interview is to explore the benefits derived from each of the important attributes. Often those who have never conducted a laddering interview are surprised to learn that it consists primarily of standard, albeit thoughtful, open-ended probes, and not, for the most part, alternative techniques. No bells and whistles! So how is it different from any other qualitative interview? The essential difference—and it's an important one—is the higher degree to which responses are probed when laddering: all the way to Rokeach!

In this step, attributes are discussed individually and benefit chains are developed. The goal is to uncover why each derived benefit is important. In practice, however, continually asking "why" is ineffective. To prove the point, try this experiment. Ask a friend for one thing

she likes about her brand of coffee and *why* that's important. Now *every time* you get an answer, ask *why* that's important. Don't stop. Be persistent!

How did it go? How far did you get? Did your friend inflict any bodily damage on you? The point is, that the "why" question is annoying and potentially confrontational. It's also lame because, if it works at all, it will more than likely produce only rational responses. NOT GOOD, since the whole reason for doing laddering is to go beyond the rational. But don't worry, there is a solution.

Alternative open-ended probes such as those listed below are more likely to produce a thoughtful, honest, and insightful response—a higher benefit level response. Try:

- **Evoking a situational context**
  "When does that occur?"
  "How does it affect the situation?"

- Postulating the absence of an object or state of being

    "What if it wasn't there?"

    "What if that did not result?"

- Addressing the disadvantage then probing for its opposite

    "For what reason wouldn't you want X?"

- Requesting changes over time

    "Was it always that way?"

    "How was it different when . . . ?"

- Shifting perspective to the third-person

    "How would others feel?"

- Checking for clarification

    "What did you mean when you said . . . ?"

- Re-directing through silence or repetition of response.

Are you up for continuing our little experiment? First, ply your friend with gifts to make up for your previous "why" badgering. Next, investigate coffee preferences utilizing the probes just listed.

How did it go this time? Did you climb all the way to Rokeach? Was your friend shocked and amazed that she held such deep-seated beliefs about coffee? You, my friend, have cracked the code. You're a ladderer in the making!

And you're ready for the final rung!

THE ANALYSIS

The ladders generated in the individual interviews are aggregated to compile one overall benefit-structure. If you like puzzle-solving, you'll love putting ladders together! It requires some sleuthing, some connecting the pieces—and an occasional use of scissors to make certain pieces fit (aka, enlightened subjectivity).

Here's a hypothetical benefit-structure of diet soft drinks. Though we weren't actually paid to conduct this study, we role-played the parts of client, interviewer, and respondent. (see "Hats" in Chapter 4.) We even ate M&M's while we were doing it. How authentic is that?

Hypothetical Benefit–Structure of Diet Soft drinks

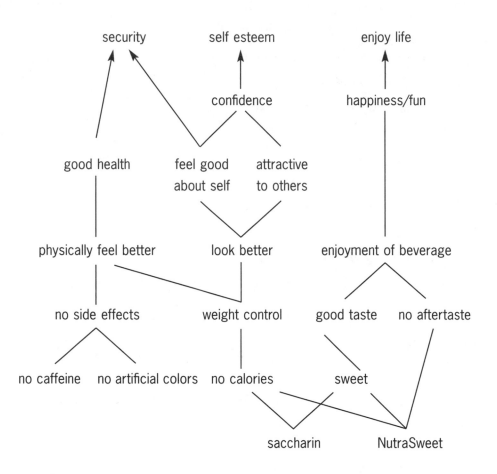

Before explaining the ladder, it will be necessary to dash the hopes of some (okay, most) hopeful clients. That's because the benefit-structure applies to the category, and thus is not exclusive to any individual brand. To the extent that product attributes are common across the category, so too is the resulting benefit-structure. Even new or unique attributes typically result in benefits that are already present within the existing structure. Take the diet soft drink example. NutraSweet, when introduced, did not produce a unique benefit chain. It merely linked into one that was already present: good taste and enjoyment of beverage. You might say that the structure is the category's reason for being and consequently, all competitive players' reason for being. And that's really okay, as you'll see if your dashed hopes allow you to read on.

This diet soft drink schematic shows an interesting historical example of how brands differentiate themselves within the category. In the early days of diet soft drinks (remember Tab?), the common positioning for most brands reflected the center benefit chain. Think back to all those gorgeous swim suit models, diet soft drinks in hand, walking seductively past armies of admiring young men on the beach.

Then along came NutraSweet, a superior tasting sugar substitute, and with it Diet Coke—surprisingly, one of the last entries in the diet soft drink category. Diet Coke differentiated itself from the competition by basing its positioning on taste and enjoyment: "Just for the taste of it . . . Diet Coke!" While other brands were soon to incorporate NutraSweet in their formulations, only Diet Coke established—and, yes, owned—the taste/enjoyment positioning.

This example also shows the wisdom of positioning at the benefit rather than the attribute level. Product attributes—even breakthrough ingredients like NutraSweet—are vulnerable and non-sustainable. While Diet Coke may have been the first to introduce NutraSweet, it wasn't long before other brands were using it as well. Furthermore, product attributes do not affect brand image, an essential element of brand equity. Only benefits, specifically higher order benefits, can do this. Why? Because they're more important to consumers and because they are more interestingly and emotionally executed. Enter the emotional connection. How many personally relevant, emotional ways can you communicate NutraSweet? Compare that to the number of ways and the depth of emotion that can be achieved when executing enjoyment, happiness, and fun. Is it any wonder that smart marketers leverage higher-level benefits when positioning their brands?

CHOOSING STRATEGIC OPTIONS

With more than one benefit chain available as strategic options, how do you choose the best, most effective one for the brand?

Back to the diet soft drink example. In broad strokes, there are three primary chains:

- **Good health**
- **Attractive to opposite sex**
- **Good taste**

The appropriateness of the positioning is dependent upon three factors:

- **Product/brand capability (Can it actually deliver?)**
- **The level of consumer importance (Does the benefit address a significant need?)**
- **The competitive environment (Does it differentiate the brand from the competition?)**

Let's take a look at each of these in the case of Diet Coke.

- **Is the product capable of delivering good taste?**

  Yes, it contains a superior sweetener, *and* it also has the heritage of good taste from its parent brand, Coke.

- **Is "good taste" a significant consumer need?**

  Yes, especially for diet soft drinks, frequently considered the poor step-children of "regular" soft drinks.

- **Is "good taste" a differentiating positioning vis-á-vis the competitive environment?**

  Yes, the competitors are all busy showing everyone how to attract the opposite sex!

There you have it. Diet Coke chose a branch on the ladder that offered them a powerful and sustainable positioning. And that's the potential of laddering!

CHAPTER 3

Exploring Emotions, Imagery, and Associations— "Projectives" and the Use of Metaphor

(Or: What animal are you feeling like today?)

S o now you're ready to go deeper still, to feelings and imagery. But how do you get people to talk about their feelings, especially when you just met them 35 minutes ago? Projective techniques are just what the moderator ordered.

PROJECTIVE OR METAPHORICAL?

Are They Projective Techniques?

"Projective techniques" is a term that is bandied about the qualitative world and is often used for everything we do beyond the introductions and opening question—all the tools and the kitchen sink too! Our view is a bit more precise. All of these techniques have to do with asking respondents to talk about one concept (e.g., brand) in light of another concept (e.g., types of flowers or automobiles).

The term "projective" comes from the field of clinical psychology. In some kinds of personality testing, ambiguous stimuli are shown to people who then tell stories based on what they see. The Thematic Apperception Test (TAT) uses vague pictures, while the Rorschach uses inkblots as stimuli. The theory goes that aspects of the individuals' personalities are revealed as they "project" feelings and desires onto stimuli. Projective techniques in qualitative research also use ambiguous stimuli, those that can be interpreted by respondents in a variety of ways to elicit feelings and images. But are our respondents really "projecting" thoughts and feelings, or is there something else going on?

Are They Metaphorical Techniques?

"You don't see something until you have the right metaphor to let you perceive it."
                                                              —Thomas Kuhn

The more appropriate name for these tools may well be "Metaphorical Techniques." And here's why. Typically, we use this set of techniques to explore an abstract concept, such as a brand's image or a life experience, in terms of a more concrete concept, such as a photograph of a specific object or scene. This is essentially metaphor. (Kövecses, 2002) Metaphorical thinking is explaining one concept in light of a second concept in order to bring new understanding and insight to the first concept.

Metaphor is used commonly in our thought and our language, probably more often than we are aware. For example, what do the following statements bring to your mind?

- *My day was a real rollercoaster.*
- *She wears her heart on her sleeve.*
- *The exam was a piece of cake.*
- *My teacher is a real battleaxe.*

But enough about you. Here's what they brought to our minds:

- *A day of ups and downs*
- *No hidden emotions with her.*
- *An easy test.*
- *The teacher from . . . well, you know.*

The bottom line is that, through the use of metaphor, these examples have conveyed meaning, emotion, and imagery. And by the way, they have done so quickly, succinctly, and powerfully. Therein lies the beauty of using these "metaphorical techniques" as the vehicle through which participants discuss their innermost feelings. Insight is conveyed in a concise and compelling way.

When using these techniques, we typically instruct respondents to *"make connections"* between a general concept and the stimuli at hand, or to *"associate"* their thoughts and feelings; *"to imagine,"* or *"to play along"* in talking about the subject in a different way. Sounds like metaphor, doesn't it?

GOING DEEP

Why do metaphorical techniques allow us to go below the surface? How do they help respondents access and articulate feelings and images that they have trouble voicing when asked in a standard question-and-answer format? One possible explanation is that the metaphorical process—that of making connections—taps into the right side of the brain. This is the creative side of the brain, where feelings and visual imagery reside. Thus, metaphorical techniques assist respondents in accessing emotions, perceptions, and imagery, allowing them to verbalize rich information that adds insight and understanding to the topic under discussion.

GOING WIDE

The abstract concept that we are trying to explain through the use of these tools is often multi-faceted. A brand or company image, for example, is not a singular idea, but rather, is likely to have a number of dimensions. Thus, multiple metaphors are often appropriate and in fact desirable, because they teach us about the different facets of the concept at hand. This argues for using a variety of stimuli within any one exercise (e.g., multiple analogies or a varied picture deck), or using more than one technique when exploring an important concept. Similarly, different sensory modalities can be tapped in order to further consider the various dimensions of the concept (e.g., not only exploring the more common visual and verbal modalities, but also using sounds, smells or textures).

Conceptual Metaphors and "Archtypal Images"

As you contemplate the individual metaphors that respondents offer you for your brand, consider that a higher order, conceptual metaphor might tie them together, providing an analytic gold nugget. Perhaps your brand is all about the hero's journey, perhaps it embodies passion with the intensity of fire, or perhaps its essence springs from the world of nature and the concept of birth, death and rebirth.

Many of these conceptual metaphors are age-old, and are full of rich meaning and deep emotion. In fact, psychologist Carl Jung (1964) might call these "archetypal images" or symbols, and would suggest that they are manifestations of deep archetypes or primordial images that span cultures and history. According to Jung, these primordial images emerge from our "collective unconscious," and are shared by all of humanity.[1]

Whether or not you agree with Jung about the collective unconscious, it is easy to perceive the power in such imagery. A search of ancient mythology, of literature through the ages, and even of the internet today will provide you with examples of these fertile symbols. So, as you examine the images articulated by respondents, you might want to see if more than a few point to a classic image, such as those that follow, in order to assist you in maximizing your brand's potential (Mark & Pearson, 2001):

CHARACTERS	SITUATIONS	SYMBOLS
Alpha-male	Adventure	Air, earth, fire or water
Crone, or wise woman	Chase/Hunt	Buildings/architecture
Fool	Creation	Light
Hero	Evolution	Road/pathway
Lover	Harvest	Snake
Mother	Healing	Sun, engine (source of power)
Poet	Initiation	Treasure
Outcast	Renewal	
Scholar	Salvation	
Warrior	Task	
	Quest	

---

1. *Not all higher order, conceptual metaphors are likely to derive from deep seated archetypes or be linked to age-old imagery. We leave it to your judgment which you choose to call "archetypal."*

METAPHOR IN ADVERTISING

Many successful ads use metaphor to communicate their brand's message. Take, for example, Coke's use of the polar bear to convey cold, refreshing, and comfort. Or Chevy Trucks' "Like A Rock" to communicate rugged strength and durability. Incorporating metaphorical techniques into your research projects may not only lead to greater understanding of your brand, but also provide a springboard for powerful advertising.

Just one more thought. Linguists have discovered that many metaphors are universal, crossing cultures and languages. In this day of global advertising, imagine discovering a universal metaphor to speak for your brand.

PROCESS TIPS FOR METAPHORICAL TECHNIQUES

Overall, participants are likely to feel more comfortable when the stimulus materials are tangible or concrete. For example, it may be easier for them to work with a picture deck than to do their own drawing. One implication of this is that you may want to save techniques that require respondents to use their own imaginations until later in the group, after rapport has been established.

When giving instructions for any of these techniques, it is often helpful to give examples using an unrelated topic.

Heads up! Think about the time involved for each exercise, and plan accordingly. When using a number of these tools, consider recruiting fewer respondents per group or conducting longer groups, so that there is ample time for each person to uncover his or her associations and images, to reflect, and to share any thoughts and interpretations during debriefs.

OVERVIEW OF METAPHORICAL TOOLS

A wide variety of stimuli can be used to encourage metaphorical thinking, and this chapter describes their range and use. Analogies are probably the most familiar, and so we start with these. Personification is another common form of metaphor, and we follow with two versions of this:

- One asks respondents to imagine that the product or brand has come alive as a person

- The other has respondents imagining a group of brands interacting in a social setting, such as at a party or within a family.

Stimuli are often visual as well. Thus we frequently use pictures to provoke metaphorical thinking, asking respondents:

- To look at pictures that we provide in tools such as **Picture Sorts** and **Collage**.

- To create their own pictures that then become the pathway to associations and metaphor. **Metaphorical Drawing, Pass the Doodle,** and **Draw the User** are three such techniques.

Other sensory modalities are less commonly used in qualitative research. However, we challenge you to consider ways in which using sounds, smells, and textures will stretch both you and your respondents, leading you to fresh ideas and imagery. We discuss some ways of exploring different sense modalities in the section on Sensory Decks.

Whichever techniques you choose, the key is that using them helps respondents to access and talk about their emotions, imagery, and associations, thereby providing the means to your unlocking the treasure, the path to the end of the rainbow, the stairway to heaven, the . . . well, you get the idea!

ANALOGIES

Analogies are the most obvious form of metaphor, so easy that they typically slip into our everyday conversations. You know, like when you're "hungry as a horse" (especially after your third group, it's 10 p.m., and you've missed lunch *and* dinner). Very simply, analogies involve asking participants to think about the issue at hand by using a different frame of reference.

When	Use when the need is to learn about perceptions of imagery related to a brand, product, issue, or service.
Task	To use an example from "another world" that corresponds in some respect to the topic.
Supplies	None
Directions	Ask respondents individually to select something from "another world" that seems similar to or shares some similar characteristics with the topic.

"If X were a (n) _____, what would it be?"

It is often helpful to use more than one analogy in a study because respondents may relate to some analogies and not to others. For example, someone might be able to provide analogies from the world of animals but not from the world of music. Also consider possible gender differences when choosing "worlds." Men may be better able to play in the arena of cars, while women may have an easier time with department stores.

"Other worlds" are limitless. Some examples:

Animal	Political party
Automobile	Type of music
Department store	Sport or team
Brand of ice cream	Type of footwear

Alternatively, you can let them choose their own world in which to play—whatever makes sense for them based on their hobbies, interests, or lifestyles. Like the guy who compared his shaving cream to a fishing lure!

Debrief   Ask respondents to explain their analogies. Some
             sample probes:

             "What is it about _____ that reminds you of X?"
             "How do the qualities of _____ seem similar to X?"
             *"What are the characteristics of _____ in its world . . . and how
             is X like that?"*

             When you solicit multiple analogies, it is more manage-
             able as well as more insightful if you allow an individual
             to explain *all* of his or her analogies for a given brand,
             and then discuss the composite image. Asking *all* the
             respondents in the group to tell what they chose as an
             animal for the brand, and then what they all chose as a
             style of music for the brand, etc., tends to be choppy and
             lacks clarity.

Variation   This is also a good exercise for understanding the
             relationship between brands. In fact, it's a smart idea
             when using analogy to compare two or more brands
             because that way you can better distinguish between
             category imagery (common to all brands) and that
             which is specific to one or the other.

Example **Project Objective:** To understand the difference
             between Coke and Pepsi, using the world of
             animals as an analogy:

             One respondent's analogy:
             *"Pepsi is a cheetah, always on the move, always fast—a cat
             that can be aggressive. Coke is still in the cat family, but he's the
             king of the jungle, the lion—powerful and secure in his
             position. A lion can fight when it wants to, but waits until it's
             attacked rather than being so aggressive."*

PERSONIFICATION

When	Use when it's important to better understand the characteristics and image of a brand, product, or service.
Task	To assign human characteristics to a brand.
Supplies	None
Directions	Ask respondents to think about the characteristics and qualities of the brand. Be clear that this exercise is about translating various characteristics or images of a brand into a representative persona. In other words, you don't want them to confuse a profile of the user with the imagery of the brand. You might say:

- *"Imagine those traits being embodied in a person. Please note that I'm not asking about who uses the product. I'm asking you to imagine that the brand has all the characteristics you've described and actually turns into a person. What kind of person would this brand be? Get an image of one particular person in your mind."*

- *"Now I'm going to ask some questions, and I'd like you to jot down what you see in your mind's eye. Don't censor your thoughts. Be as specific as you can. And if you don't have a particular answer in mind, don't worry, just wait and answer the next one. We're trying to get a well-rounded picture of the person you've envisioned X to be."*

Sample probes:

Physical Characteristics

These are pretty easy for respondents to anchor to a specific "brand." Don't allow ranges in age, however. They should have a single individual in mind. Stress again that it's not about users or whether they personally like or don't like the brand.

- *"Male or female?"*
- *"How old?"*
- *"What size or shape?"*

Descriptions and Preferences

Respondents will begin describing choices their "person" might make, which can give insight into how they perceive the brand.

- *"What is this person wearing?"*
- *"What style of clothes?"*
- *"What hair style?"*
- *"What does this person do during the day?"*
- *"Is this person employed or unemployed?"*
- *"Is this person in school?"*
- *"Does this person do something else?"*
- *"What kind of car does this person drive?"*
- *"What is this person's home life like?"*
- *"Married?"*
- *"Single?"*
- *"Kids?"*
- *"Pets?"*
- *"What does this person like to do with any spare time?"*
- *"What TV show and/or website does this person like?"*
- *"Favorite song? Artist? Radio station?"*
- *"What's this person's favorite reading material?"*

Philosophy:

Quick questions can help you understand important issues, stances, or views the "person" has.

- *"How does this person feel about his or her life right now?"*
- *"What is this person proud of?"*
- *"What's this person's goal? What is he or she looking forward to most?"*
- *"What's this person's motto in life?"*

Topping It Off:

This adds an extra degree of dimension—and fun!

- *"What's this person's name or nickname?"*

Debrief   Invite volunteers to share a description of the person they envisioned, using the details they selected. As a moderator, you're looking for an understanding of the various facets of the "person."

Here's an interesting probe: *"If you met this person in a social situation, would it be someone you'd want to spend time with or might you avoid them?"*

Get comparisons from the rest of the group:

"Did anyone else have something similar?" or

"Did anyone have something completely different?"

After all respondents have explained their characters, ask the group to play back common themes. Ask what it is about the brand that had several people thinking along the same lines. Be sure to probe if this is a positive or negative characteristic within the category.

Hint
Sometimes walking the group through an unrelated example can work well to establish your expectations for this exercise. You can start off by giving them *your* thoughts about how the characteristics *you* associate with unrelated companies might be turned into a person, and then throw it open to the group for more details. An example might help here:

"If someone asked me to consider the differences between Macintosh and IBM computers, I'd say I think of Macintosh as being rather creative and rather brave in challenging the status quo, but still businesslike. So, the person I see is a young businessman, about 32. He's got longish red hair and a great smile. He's wearing a jacket and a crisp white shirt, jeans, and loafers with no socks."

"In comparison, I see IBM as an older, successful businessman. He's dressed in a dark suit, all buttoned up. He's very sophisticated, has a little gray at the temples. And he's a very smart businessman. He's curious to learn what 'Mac' has up his sleeve. What do you think IBM's name would be? What kind of car would you see this IBM-Person driving? Where do you think he vacations?"

*"Okay, get the idea about turning characteristics into a person? I'm not describing **who** I think uses a Mac or an IBM computer. I'm really focussed on what kind of person the company would be if it came to life."*

"Now I'd like you to do this for two of the brands we've been talking about—Toyota and Luxus."

Another hint   Respondents can have a difficult time leaving behind the personality of a company spokesperson or icon. When doing this exercise for fast food outlets, for example, McDonald's could easily emerge as a clown á la Ronald, and Burger King could be depicted as royalty. In this case, you may have more success with a different metaphorical exercise. Perhaps offer pictures or categories from which they can choose—obviously avoiding any circus, clown, or royalty pictures in the above cited case.

Variation   As in analogies, it's very helpful to have respondents personify two brands and compare and contrast the two "individuals." You may also probe any interaction that might occur between these two "people," which leads us to the next tool, Party/Family of Brands.

PARTY/FAMILY OF BRANDS

In real life, social gatherings are rife with subtle and not-so-subtle pos-
turing. Relationships can be identified and are played out for all the
world to see. Have you ever discovered some hidden agenda or an
interesting personality trait by being a fly-on-the-wall and observing
what happens around you? Imagine what that fly could tell about
how family members or office co-workers really interact with each
other. What better way for uncovering the relationships that exist
between brands or products than by expanding personification to
cover social interactions?

When	Use during category exploration, with a need to know the relationship that exists between different brands. Or if you have a brand that has different product offerings and you want to understand the relationship between them. This could help to determine where a new addition might fit or if there's a disconnect among certain products in the portfolio.
Task	To tell a story about the key players. It could be in the context of family or another social group, such as people at a party. The story can be acted out or simply told to the group.
Supplies	An item to represent each of the key brands. These may be actual products, such as bottles of soft drinks or empty ice cream containers, or you could use either tent cards with the names of the key brands on them or index cards on which are pasted appropriate company logos.

Version A: Party

Directions   Ask respondents to imagine that there's a party going on.
Then instruct them as follows:

- *"Think about what happens at a party. Someone hosts it. Some guests arrive early; others arrive late. Some have lots of fun; some are quiet; there's mingling going on."*

- *"Here are the players."* (Give each respondent a set, or ask the group to focus on a single set of stimuli—products, packages, logos—placed on the table or easel.)

- *"Based upon your impressions of each brand and working independently, take two minutes to think about what would be happening at this party. Write down some notes if it's helpful. Cast each brand as a character at the party. Who's doing what? Who's talking to whom? Who's the life of the party? Who's not having fun?"* (You can create your own probes to fit your objectives, such as: *"Who's wearing what?"* or *"What's the theme of the party?"* or *"What kind of music is being played?"*, etc.)

- *"At the end of two to three minutes, you'll present your vision of the party to the rest of the group."*

Version B: Family

Tell respondents to think about relationships that can develop within an extended family.

- *"Think about different relationships. Mother, father, kids are pretty obvious. There are grandparents and aunts and uncles. Who else can there be in extended families? Long-lost cousins; black sheep; steps and in-laws. And, people can have different personalities, like the rebellious teen, the studious child, the industrious brother, or the slacker."*
- *"Here are the family members."* (Give each person a set, or ask them to focus on the stimuli you have on the table.)
- *"Based upon your impressions of each brand and working individually, take two minutes and think about which brand represents which family member and jot down your ideas. Consider who's in charge. Who's **really** running the show? Who influences whom?"*
- *"At the end of two to three minutes, you'll present your vision of this family to the rest of the group."*

Debrief   Allow each person to explain what was envisioned. Probe for clarification and detail so that you understand their brand perceptions.

Once everyone has shared, ask the group if they heard common themes. Probe for the rationale behind themes. You can also go back and probe two different stories if a key brand was played out differently. For example, you could ask, *"What is it about the brand that made one person see it this way and someone else see it that way?"*

Example   **Project Objective:** Back in the early 1990s, Absolut Vodka had just introduced its lemon, orange, and pepper vodka line extensions. Prior to introducing the currant flavored version, they wanted to learn how consumers might see this fitting into the "family" of Absolut Vodkas.

	Absolut Original	Absolut Citron	Absolut Peppar	Absolut Kurant
Family member	Parent, Father	Mother, Sibling	Child, Teenager	Baby (girl), Sibling
Image	Strong, Patriarch	Alluring, Sweet	Rebel, Wild	Sweet, Soft
Role in the portfolio	Base of family	Broad appeal	"Hot"	New addition

Variations   Depending on your topic and your target, you could change the setting to that of a work group, a fire department putting out a fire, a sports team, a town, etc.

Hint   Allow pairs of respondents to work together in creating a party or family. Sometimes sharing a creative endeavor is less threatening. It also takes less time for four pairs to tell their stories than for eight individuals to tell theirs. Bear in mind that one person in the pair will probably do most of the explaining, but you can probe to make sure that it represents both points of view.

METAPHORICAL DRAWING

Drawing, even when it's no more than stick-figure quality, is a wonderful way of allowing respondents to access a different part of the brain, expressing their feelings and perceptions via visual rendering. Drawing permits a less rational, more emotional reaction—one that respondents may be unable to justify (nor should they be expected to if it's just a gut feeling), but one that has the potential of going below the surface of issues or beliefs that are difficult to articulate.

When   Use when the objective is to understand more detail about a situation, relationship, or image.

Task   To draw a picture that represents the category or topic under exploration.

Supplies   Plain paper (at least 8 ½" x 11"); fineline colored markers.

Supply Tip

When conducting any drawing exercise, be sure that you have good quality supplies available (paper, markers, colored pencils), and always encourage respondents to use multiple colors. We've found that they tend to become more involved in the task and are likely to produce a more insightful drawing when "honored" with choice materials.

We've also discovered that, compared to pen or pencil markings, colored markers tend to show up better when held up for viewing in the group and when scanning or copying for the report.

Directions   Tell respondents they will be drawing stick figures or shapes and symbols to represent how they perceive the category. Give them a time frame (usually about five minutes). Show them some examples of symbols by drawing some yourself on the easel. For example, simple smiley faces could be people, a circle with stick underneath could be a tree, a rectangle could be a car. And invite them to label anything they think might be unclear or misinterpreted.

- Tell respondents to think about the different players in the category and how they relate to each other. You might want to give some examples, depending upon the category, such as *"Who's bigger than whom?"* or *"Who's pushing an idea and who's resisting it?"* or *"How would you draw the competition between X, Y, and Z?"* or *"Who's winning, who's gaining ground?"*

- Consider asking respondents to think metaphorically to show the relationship. For instance, use another world such as underwater sea life, outer space, or an operating room.

Process Tip

Allay any angst about drawing ability by telling respondents that you expect, and actually prefer, no more than stick-figure quality.

Example   **Project Objective:** To assess how the general public perceives the relative strength or position of the various long distance providers in order to create advertising that is consistent with current perceptions. (This project was conducted in the early 1990s when long distance carriers were fighting to gain and retain customers.)

Debrief of one respondent's drawing:

"AT&T is a giant tree that's been growing forever. MCI and Sprint are attacking the tree. MCI has a chainsaw and can do a lot more damage than Sprint can with just his axe. All the other resellers are picking away at the tree, but aren't really having much affect . . . . they're just waiting for MCI and Sprint to chop the tree down first, making it easier for them to get at it. So far, AT&T is still standing, but maybe not for long."

Variation

When you're working with intangible topics like services or issues, consider using a symbol—like a red sticky dot—to represent the service or issue in the drawing. Ask respondents to incorporate the dot into their pictures, showing their feelings toward or relationship with it. This way, it's easy to key in on the service or issue as you look across the different drawings, despite the variety of contexts chosen by different respondents.

BASIC PICTURE DECKS

A picture is worth a thousand words. Or in this case, it's the start of a thousand words when respondents use pictures as metaphors to describe their perceptions. Using an assortment of pictures is simply another kind of analogy exercise that can help respondents think more broadly through forced connections. The pictures in a moderator's deck are another way of providing a world in which respondents can "play."

When   Use when the need is to learn about the imagery or emotional associations respondents have about a brand, experience, or issue.

Task   To select a picture that best represents the image or feeling associated with the topic.

Supplies   An assortment of pictures that represent a wide range of images, emotions, or feelings. Because the pictures you choose set the parameters for respondents' connections, care should be taken to insure the deck is objective and broad. Some tips for selecting a deck:

- Represent a wide range of possibilities. For each picture you choose, challenge yourself to find an opposite image or feeling to insure a broad spectrum.

- Make sure the pictures aren't bland. They must evoke feelings and images in order to serve their purpose. A picture that draws you in to look further or see more is far more effective than one that simply shows a model in a sterile context.

- Do not include pictures that are related to the topic in any way (e.g., avoid pictures of kids or kitchens when exploring play kitchens) because these will produce only literal or rational responses.

- Have a consistent format. All pictures should be about the same size and quality (e.g., all either laminated, in sheet protectors or mounted on cardboard), so that they aren't chosen simply because of their superior quality.

- Code the stimuli because when talking with respondents you're less likely to project your own interpretation of pictures if you simply refer to them by their codes. As an example, it's better that you refer to the picture as A-22 than "the ferocious lion," especially if ferocity is not why the respondent selected the picture.

Directions
Tell respondents that they will be looking at a collection of pictures that represent a wide variety of feelings, attitudes, and images. Be specific in the language you use when instructing the respondents—language that reflects the purpose of the exercise:

- *"Review all the pictures, looking at the feeling, emotion, or attitude that each one represents."*

- *"Choose one that best represents X to you (e.g., "the attitude you associate with Coca-Cola", or "the feeling you have when riding a train," or "what American Airlines stands for").*

- *"Make a note of the code number of the picture chosen."*

Debrief
Ask one volunteer to:

- *"Describe your chosen picture."*

- *"Tell about the connections or associations that you made."*

Then ask if anyone else in the group chose the same picture. Find out if it was chosen for a different reason, and encourage additional connections.

Variation 1
Ask respondents to think about two brands and then choose a picture that best represents each one. You might choose to do this if you're interested in:

- A product or brand's competitive set.

- The old and new version.

- Comparing and contrasting two kinds of usage occasions or experiences, such as the difference in perceptions of various forms of public transportation —bus and train or taxi and subway.

When debriefing, allow each respondent to compare and contrast his or her selections before moving on to the next person.

Variation 2   Have respondents choose multiple pictures (perhaps representing multiple facets or different kinds of associations) for a topic. Put all of one individual's pictures on an easel sheet and then ask that person or the group to sum up what is seen.

Variation 3   Give all respondents their own (but identical) picture decks to sort through, and ask them to sort the pictures based upon "fit" or "no fit." Ask them what all the "fit" pictures have in common, or ask them to identify common themes they see emerging in their "fit" pile.

Alternatively, have the group do it as a whole, especially if the budget for producing individual decks is a concern.

ALTERNATIVE TYPES OF PICTURE DECKS

Users

Offer pictures showing people of different ages, different lifestyles, and different ethnic backgrounds to represent users. You may want only individuals, or you may want a mix of individuals, families, social groups, and/or work groups. As always, challenge your own assumptions, and insure that your deck is broad enough to encourage diverse opinions to emerge.

Evocative

Many ads have pictures that "tell a story" on their own (e.g., a bullfighter who's down but the bull is looking away; a mother peering out a window at children playing; a man and a woman talking to each other in a restaurant). A collection of these kinds of images can help respondents tell a story rather than just relate simple, descriptive words or phrases. Because there tends to be a wider interpretation for these types of pictures, there can be more depth of response.

Homogeneous Decks

Try using a deck of like objects, such as a deck with all animals, or all chairs, or all shoes, or all hairstyles. You could assemble a deck with pictures of nature in general or a deck with just trees. It's nice to have some collections on hand, but there are times when a particular project may provoke a need or idea for a new homogeneous deck.

For example, if your objective is to understand what role a new product or service might play, try collecting a deck of pictures showing tools ranging from a dentist's drill to a tire jack, from a backhoe to a knitting needle. Then talk about what kind of "tool" the new product or service is, and discuss its role from that standpoint.

A celebrity deck is effective if you're dealing with a topic that has personality characteristics, since celebrities embody specific, identifiable traits. Imagine explaining a brand's personality in terms of its similarity to Madonna vs. Britney Spears or Cleopatra vs. Madame Curie! Care should be taken to select celebrities who are well-known to your respondents so that no one feels excluded or ignorant, and so respondents don't limit their choices to the few faces they recognize.

Pre-Existing Decks

To create decks that are almost ready-made, learn the art of borrowing from other disciplines:

- Teaching supplies (e.g., flash cards with simple, consistent pictures)

- Board games (e.g., cards from the game Masterpiece are copies of well-known works of art, all of which have different emotions or stories to project).

- Books (Those coffee table books that are typically on sale at bookstores for $5–10 often contain some very interesting images).

- Calendars (Look for the ones on sale in February or March).

Supply Tips

Ask others, including children or parents, to help you by keeping their eyes open for provocative or specific pictures. There are many online sources available today that can help you search for and download particular images for your picture deck. *Microsoft Gallery* is one we've used. You can put in a request for a photograph of the Pope or a clip art picture of a kettle to round out a deck. You can even use clip art to create an entire deck.

Video Decks

Show respondents a variety of video clips—but without sound because dialogue and/or music limits respondents' own personal interpretations and connections. These clips could be famous scenes from films, TV shows, cartoons, or commercials. Use your imagination. After each clip, ask respondents to jot down how (or if) it connects to the topic at hand. Begin the debrief by asking for the strongest connections.

Sensory Decks

While pictures are the most common stimuli, many other types of sensory stimuli could and have been used as well. In fact, any ambiguous stimulus that touches the senses could be used in a metaphorical exercise.

Scents have the possibility of evoking deep-seated emotions. Consider providing a variety of scents and posing the question, *"If this brand were a scent, what scent would it be?"*

In addition to visual stimuli such as traditional picture decks or the impact of scents, an inventive moderator might consider using:

- Cuts of music

- Musical instruments

- Different colors

- Differently textured objects

- Different tastes

Note: Don't use different tastes as a taste test, though. Use different tastes as stimuli to evoke or provoke images, moods, or memories. Remember, it's not about the stimuli specifically; it's about what the stimuli conjure up in the respondents—the connections they can make to the topic.

COLLAGE

A collage is a collection of pictures, words, symbols, or other materials that, when combined, create an image or an overall feeling about the topic at hand.

When	Use when the purpose is to explore imagery or to encourage deeper reflection on a brand, topic, experience, or issue.
Task	To create a collage representing images, feelings, and associations.
Supplies	Magazines, markers, scissors, glue, and paper for mounting.
	Optional art supplies can include ribbon, stickers, cloth, tissue, wrapping paper, etc.
Hints	• Plan on enough magazines so people have a choice to work from. We usually offer 12–16 magazines for a group of 8 respondents.
	• Select magazines that are unrelated to the topic so as to force metaphorical thinking.
	• Fashion magazines do not typically yield a wide variety of pictures. Try searching for different kinds of magazines that might represent different points of view, ages, lifestyles, activities, locations, and topics.
	• Magazines catering to photography buffs are wonderful sources for different kinds of images, although they're typically more expensive than others.
Directions	Ask respondents to create a collage, using the supplies provided, that visually represents the images, feelings, and associations they have about X.

Process Tip

Write the assignment on the easel for respondents to review as they get absorbed in the project. This will help them stay focused on the objective.

Encourage them to use symbols as opposed to literal depictions. For example, if the assignment is to create a collage on parenting, it would be preferable for respondents to select pictures that are metaphors for their feelings as opposed to simply an array of parent/child pictures. In fact, you might even tell them not to include any pictures of parents or children.

Time box this task. Allow a total of 15-20 minutes for creating the collage, and notify the group of elapsed time every five minutes. During the last five-minute period, ask respondents to finish and clean up.

Remove all materials from the table prior to presentation of collages so as to eliminate distractions.

When finished, ask respondents to title their collages. This provides them with an opportunity to reflect upon their work and summarize their intentions fairly succinctly, making it easier to understand their connections to the topic.

Debrief   In random or "popcorn" fashion—based upon who would like to share first—ask respondents to describe their collages, including the meaning and significance of the words, symbols, and pictures selected.

After all collages have been presented, ask respondents to identify common themes and to reflect on differences and surprises.

Example   **Project Objective: To understand the process of losing weight, including the thoughts and feelings surrounding weight loss.**

Collage:
Before

Debrief of Collages:

Before losing weight—*"I've lost 25 lbs. Before I lost the weight, I hated the way I looked in photographs, I'd wear big clothes to hide my hips, and I was always scolding myself about getting it together to lose weight. I found it really difficult to get motivated to lose the weight. I was always 'going to' get around to it. It was depressing all around. Maybe most importantly, I wasn't paying attention to my health. That's what the cows represent, 'cause I ate more meat and higher fat foods back then."*

Collage:
After

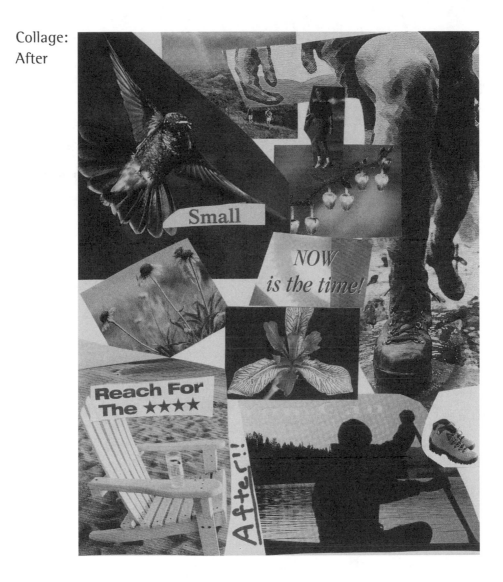

After losing weight—*"Losing the weight is, well I can only describe it as empowering. I have this feeling that I did this, and I've kept it off for a year and what's my next challenge?! I feel in charge of my health (that's what the Echinacea flowers represent), in charge of my life even. I'm more at peace with myself (see the chair by the water), but it's also a day in and day out vigilance. I put 'Now is the time' because while I can loosen up a little, it's a new lifestyle and so I don't say 'oh it's the holidays, I can eat' or 'oh it's vacation, I don't have to exercise.' And this lifestyle is going to let me do the things I like to do for a long time, I hope! Like hiking and being active*

outdoors. And of course, being smaller, lighter (the hummingbird), I feel more attractive (flowers—Irises are my favorite flower). I like the way I look in my clothes. I can look at myself in pictures again!"

Variations   Allow respondents to work in pairs or teams.

Ask respondents to create two collages to compare and contrast two brands or two concepts, such as "before and after" or "reality and wish."

Ask respondents to create a collage at home prior to attending the group (see Chapter 1).

PASS THE DOODLE

Finally—an exercise that legitimizes doodling! Those random, goofy little scribbles that you often make while you're on the phone (or in a meeting) can actually become the springboard for terrific insights!

When	Use when the purpose is to gain a better understanding of consumer perceptions, feelings, or imagery relative to an issue, a product, or a brand.
Task	To create an abstract, respondent-generated image from which to access feelings.
Supplies	An 8 ½" x 11" sheet of paper for each respondent; fine-line colored markers.
Directions	Invite respondents to take a mental break from the topic—to clear their minds.

- *"I'd like you to simply doodle on your sheet of paper. Any doodle is fine: a favorite drawing, scribble, sudden inspiration. Just freewheel!"*

- After about two minutes, have respondents put their initials on the back of their papers (so they can eventually identify their own), then have them pass their doodles to the persons on their left.

- *"Now doodle on your neighbor's doodle! Extend it, add to it, give it a new direction."*

After about one minute, have respondents again pass their doodles to the persons on their left. This process continues until respondents get their original doodles back.

- *"Now as you look over your 'enhanced doodle,' find something in it that reminds you of X—shows how you think or feel about it—and share those feelings."*

Debrief	As insights are shared, ask others in the group if they have similar feelings to add to the originally expressed perception. Invite opposing viewpoints as well.

Example 1 **Project Objective:** To explore the interpersonal dynamics within Company A.

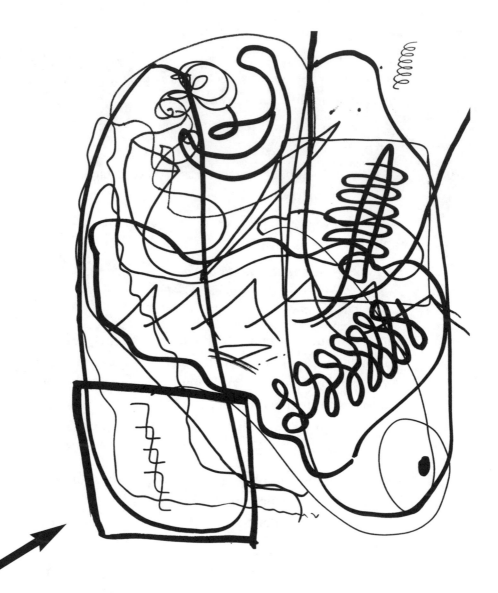

Debrief of one respondent's connection within the Doodle:

"I chose this part. What I liked about it was that everything was very connected and interdependent. But that is not how my company operates. My company is very splintered and very uncommunicative. And all the different levels of management

work totally independent of each other. It's terrible to be in it. There are some really good things about where I work. We get some really good benefits . . . but as far as the interaction between the actual employees, there's really a lot of work to be done." [Female, administrator in CPA firm]

Example 2 **Project Objective:** To explore teenagers' perceptions of and feelings about their school.

Debrief of One Respondent's Connection within the Doodle:

"I like this area here. I've always been attracted to squiggly lines. It reminded me of my school because my school's kind of wild because of how many kids are in it and how many different types of kids are in it. And all the teachers and all the stuff that goes on. A lot of kids, a lot of different aged kids, a lot of

kids with different temperments, lots of different projects. They're working on loosening the uniforms and it's just getting really wild. [Probe: is wild a good thing or a bad thing?] It's kind of both. Sometimes I really like it. It's exciting. But sometimes, like if I'm feeling tired, I don't." [Female, grade 8, aged 13]

Variation   Try a group doodle at the easel. Give each respondent a different color marker and have the group doodle in tag-team fashion. In this case, everyone uses the same doodle to access feelings.

DRAW THE USER

Having respondents imagine and draw a typical user is a way to uncover feelings, perceptions, and imagery that they associate with consumers. As participants create their drawings, the range of their perceptions is brought to mind. The resulting pictures and the symbols included offer a vehicle through which to articulate user imagery. It's almost as much fun as *Pictionary*—and less Freudian than drawing Mom!

When	Use when the objective is to gain a better understanding of consumer perceptions of users of a preferred brand or competitive brands. Importantly, these findings often shed light on brand imagery as well.

This technique can also be used to explore perceptions of:

- Particular life stages (e.g., the retiree or new dad)

- Lifestyle-specific activities (e.g., the working mom at breakfast or the empty nester on vacation)

- Participants in a specific activity (e.g., a female high school athlete or the symphony season's ticket holder)

Task	To draw step-by-step simple pictures of a given brand's typical user.
Supplies	Drawing paper (at least 8 ½" x 11"); fineline colored markers. As with other drawing exercises, good quality materials inspire creativity and involvement. Also, darker colored markers reproduce better for a report or presentation.
Directions	Tell respondents that they will be drawing the user of X brand and ask them to follow your instructions and keep up as you give step-by-step directions. As always, reassure respondents that simple, stick-figure drawing is all that's required. Move along quickly. The entire drawing should take no more than 5–7 minutes.

- *"Draw a stick-figure outline of the body of the user, taking up the full size of the page."*

- *"Next, fill in facial features, hair, and headgear."*

- *"Now add clothing that is characteristic of the X user. Don't forget shoes!"*

- *"Place something in the user's hand to reflect lifestyle—what he or she is into."*

- *"Extend a cartoon balloon from the user's mouth, and write in a sentence or phrase that you would expect him or her to say."*

- *"Fill in any background or surroundings that would help to further describe the user or the context or situation in which the product is being used."*

- *"Finally, name the user."*

Debrief   Allow each respondent to explain his or her drawing. Probe for meanings of various elements or perceptions that were projected through the drawing.

Variation   If interested in comparing two brands, walk respon-dents through a second, competitive-user drawing, but do this prior to debriefing the first so that they are not influenced by discussion of the first drawing when executing the next. Probe for comparisons, differences, and what is suggested about the two brands or the users of the two brands.

Example   **Project Objective:** To compare and contrast the image of the GAP and the Old Navy shopper.

Debrief of one respondent's GAP drawing:

"Shanna is in her mid 20s and likes to shop at the GAP. She's kind of artsy but she's not too crazy. She's not high maintenance and doesn't wear a lot of make-up. She's educated and she loves to read. She enjoys hanging out with her friends and she likes to cook. She sticks to the basics, but she does follow the trends. She doesn't spend a lot on clothes."

Debrief of one respondent's Old Navy drawing:

*"Steph's in high school. She's very outgoing and has lots of friends. She goes to sleepovers on weekends and lives for her volleyball team. She's into Boy Bands (Backstreet Boys, *NSnyc). She really likes to be trendy but she has to buy her own clothes with her babysitting money. She checks out Old Navy almost every weekend."*

CHAPTER 4

Exploring Different Perspectives

(Or: If you could walk a mile in my shoes)

Sometimes it's helpful to encourage respondents to shift perspective, viewing a topic or issue from a different vantage point. (Sometimes it's helpful to encourage this same behavior from bosses and spouses too. Read on and just think of the possibilities!) Shifting perspective—also known as role playing—is a way of bringing different points of view about a topic to the table. Participants are asked to take a specific role, such as mother, child, or teacher, or they are asked to represent one side of an issue and then discuss the topic from that point of view. (Finally, I get to be my mother!) A range of thoughts, opinions, and feelings are thus acknowledged as potentially valid, and yet respondents are not in the position of claiming any one view point as their own during the role-play.

Following the shifting perspective exercise, a discussion ensues as participants react to the various issues and points of view that were mentioned. It's interesting to see if respondents change their initial opinions as a result of hearing different viewpoints.

Shifting perspective can be used for any topic, but may be particularly useful for research on issues that evoke strong emotions. Such emotion can be brought out in the open in a relatively objective or dispassionate way before individuals commit to it. Shifting perspective may also be used to explore the persuasiveness of different points of view, prior to the development of a public relations or advertising campaign.

113

These techniques can be especially helpful to a group that seems locked into one point of view (the group that is trapped in a downward spiral and about ready to hit the ground at 100 mph . . . Splat!). By engaging respondents in these alternative exercises, they are forced to consider other options.

The next three exercises, Word Bubbles, Hats, and Debate, are excellent examples of shifting perspective techniques. Word Bubbles are also useful when it's likely that what's being said does not correspond with true feelings—as is often the case with politically sensitive or emotionally charged issues. Word Bubbles help to get beneath the words and shed light on the conflict.

WORD BUBBLES

When   Use when it is necessary to uncover sensitive, politically incorrect, or conflicting attitudes, to obtain multiple perspectives.

Task   To compose words, thoughts, or feelings of one or more people in a given situation.

Version A—Single View

Supplies   Pre-drawn template (8 ½" x 11") including a stick figure with cartoon balloons coming from the mouth, head, and heart with a direction under each balloon.

Version B—Two Views

Supplies   Pre-drawn template (8 ½″ x 11″) including two stick figures with roles labeled (e.g., Parent and Child; Salesperson and Customer), with cartoon balloons coming from
their mouths, heads, and hearts, with a direction under
each balloon.

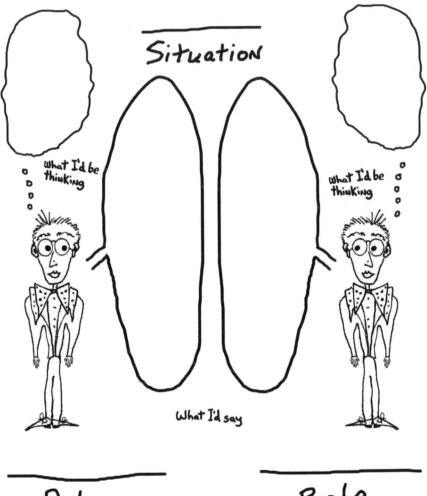

Directions   Give each respondent his or her own template drawing. Ask each to fill in the balloons privately as follows:

Version A—Single View

- What he or she would *say* about **X**, in the talk bubble coming out of the mouth.

- What he or she would really be *thinking* about **X**, in the thought bubble coming out of the head.

- What he or she would be *feeling* about **X**, in the heart bubble coming out of the body.

Version B—Two Views

- What they would be *saying* to each other about **X**.

- What they would really be *thinking* about **X**.

- What they would be *feeling* about **X**.

Debrief   If dealing with a sensitive or politically charged subject, collect drawings and read them to the group anonymously. Otherwise, you can have respondents read their own drawings. Invite group comments, using probes like these:

- *"Can anyone relate to this?"*

- *"What's happening here?"*

- *"What does this suggest about X?"*

Example 1 **Project Objective:** To better understand the thinking and emotional response of co-dependents toward the alcoholics in their lives.

Debrief of Word Bubble:

It bothers me to see her drinking so much. She looks stupid when she's drunk—she slurs her speech and makes no sense. And that's not who she really is. I'm concerned about her health, her job, her relationships. Alcohol's going to be her best friend, not me. I feel guilty because I can't get her to stop— maybe I'm not trying hard enough.

Example 2 Project Objective: To explore reactions of renters to the service received from a real estate management company.

Debrief of Word Bubble:

I feel like the landlord doesn't care about my problems. He just wants to get in and out. If he did the job right the first time, he wouldn't have to make ten trips afterwards. He does things at his own convenience. I have to sit around and wait for him; I'm on his clock. He doesn't know what it's like to be in my shoes. He has too many apartment buildings and he can't keep up with them all. I just can't count on him.

Variation   Experiment beyond stick figures with words, thoughts, and feelings. Try drawing a picture of a house with a balloon overhead that is labeled "What the family is thinking." Or draw a picture of a school labeled "What students are thinking."

Consider the key player in a situation and ask what other people in his or her life might be thinking or saying. For example, in the case of a homemaker as the key player, ask what her immediate family, her extended family, her friends, her spouse, or her neighbors are thinking or saying.

Using word bubbles, you can even elicit projected thoughts or feelings from other things—like a pet (what the pet thinks, says, or feels about a new food or a new carpet cleaner) or a car (how it would feel about a hand car wash or an automated wash). You get the idea.

HATS

When

Use when there is a need for different viewpoints and perspectives to emerge in order to explore which, if any, of these is valid for participants. This exercise allows respondents to see an issue or product from perspectives that they might not otherwise consider.

This can be especially useful for political or social issues when you need to understand vulnerabilities or potential hot buttons. It can also be helpful in new product introductions to show what other selling points, opportunities, or red flags might exist.

The Hats technique is used when there are a number of players involved with the topic, players who might have different points of view. For example:

- With a school-related topic, roles might include several children of different ages and sexes, one or more teachers, the school principal, parents, other school personnel, and a member of the school board.

- With a community related issue, roles might include elected officials, citizens, small business owners, etc.

- With a household purchase decision, players might include parents, children, a neighbor, or Fido.

Task

To give respondents a persona different from their own, asking them to speak from that perspective.

Directions

Tell respondents, *"I'm going to ask you to put on a different hat now from the one you usually wear. Respondent 1, you wear the hat of a mother of two young children. Respondent 2, a 10-year-old boy. Respondent 3, a school teacher."*

Now ask respondents to respond to the issue or idea in the way they think their characters would.

Give them a minute or two to "get into character" and think about what their positions would be. Encourage them to "be" that person for a few minutes.

Debrief   Here are some sample probes to use when the role-playing has been completed:

- *"What made sense to you?"*

- *"What could you relate to?"*

- *"Do you feel any differently now that you've heard other points of view?"* Probe for understanding.

Variations   Write the various roles ("hats") on slips of paper, and have respondents draw their roles from an actual hat! Or try giving the entire table the same role, eliciting responses, then giving them another role. Keep it fast, non-judgmental, and fun.

DEBATE

When	Use when there is a need to fully elicit the pros and cons of an issue. This technique could also be used to explore the potential benefits and barriers to a new product idea.
Task	To divide group in half, asking one half to argue the positive side of the issue and the other group to argue the negative.
Directions	Arbitrarily divide respondents into two groups, with equal numbers in each group. Give each group three to five minutes to develop its position on the issue. Ask each group to report on its discussion to the other group.
Debrief	Sample probes:

- *"How did you feel about the two points of view?"*

- *"What made sense to you?"*

- *"What could you relate to?"*

- *"Do you feel any differently now than when we started this discussion?"*

- *"What was most powerful to you?"*

Hint	Note that directions should be given in a playful tone, perhaps encouraging each side to be as convincing as possible to the other group.
Variation	Ask respondents whether they are positive or negative toward the issue, and then divide the group based on similar attitudes. Then ask each group to develop the position for the *opposite* point of view. This technique is called "Role Reversal."

CHAPTER 5

Exploring the Junk Drawer

(Or: Little treasures that just don't fit
anywhere else in the kitchen)

The surprise $20 bill in the pocket of your jeans! The ice cream bars hidden behind the frozen peas! THE GOODIES IN THE JUNK DRAWER!

Other than the fact that both of the techniques that follow start with the letter "I," they have very little in common—besides, of course, their ability to stretch your thinking about moderating. And since we have it on pretty good authority that that's why you're here anyway, read on about different approaches to introductions and the interplay between qualitative research and ideation. Prepare to streeeeeeeeeeeeeeetch even further!

THE POWER OF INTRODUCTIONS
(Or: Hello. My name is Max.)

Imagine you've been invited to a new friend's home for a party. You're poised at the door, ready to knock. You're excited, but also wondering who else is there. Are you over-dressed? Is your breath fresh? What if your friend serves those little cheese-things you're allergic to? And then the door opens and you're in, beginning to mix and mingle, and now wondering if you'll find someone there to talk to comfortably, someone you'll have something in common with, someone interesting.

All right, now imagine that same scenario, but imagine that, after the door opens, your hostess is at your side, introducing you, whispering who's who, getting you settled. All of a sudden you're relaxed and you start to enjoy yourself.

123

Similarly, the introductory period of a focus group can offer assurances by making people feel comfortable. First impressions count a lot, and this is the point at which you have the power to set the stage for the rest of the group.

For just a moment let's consider the focus group a team of sorts, with its mission to share thoughts and perceptions for the common goal of educating you about their behaviors and attitudes. According to theory on team building, specifically the Drexler Sibbet Team Performance Model, there are **four stages** of orientation for the development of a functioning team, all of which seem applicable to focus groups.

1. Orientation: Why am I here?

Respondents need to know they have a purpose for being in the group. Additionally, they want to feel that they belong. This stage is all about offering participants personal comfort via acknowledgement and appreciation. It is also about informing them what a focus group is about and how they'll be able to help.

2. Trust Building: Who are you?

Participants need to know who else is in the group and what role everyone will play in order to develop a sense of trust. This will lead to mutual regard, spontaneous interaction, and forthrightness. (Way better than passive-aggressive, right?)

As they peek at who else is sitting around the table, you can almost hear some of them thinking, "Is she a working mom?" or "Does he have gastric upset too?" Letting respondents share a little bit about their lives allows them to begin making connections with others in the group. More about ways to do this in a moment.

3. Goal Clarification: What are we doing?

In order for them to participate fully and offer greatest value, respondents need a clear understanding of the specific goals of the group discussion and their roles in it.

This is where you provide more detail about the logistics of what's going to happen and how you'd like them to behave (e.g., *"You'll be giving your opinions about new product ideas, and you should express your own opinions when you participate in the discussion. Agreement and consensus aren't necessary. In fact, I relish a range of viewpoints."*)

4. Commitment: How will we do it?

With a shared understanding of what they're being asked to do and how to do it, respondents are usually ready, willing, and able to jump right in, particularly once you've told them how they will be going about it: *"You will be retrieving information, facts, memories, feeling, and associations from within yourselves, articulating them to the group, and engaging in activities planned to help you do both these things."*

INTRODUCTORY QUESTIONS

Consider structuring your introductory questions as follows:

Create questions that are:	So that:
Easy/simple to answer	Respondents are confident in their ability to answer
A little bit challenging/revealing	Respondents practice sharing more than just surface answers
Involving for everyone	All have the ability to answer
Effective in soliciting general background information	You have a framework for interpretation
Not or only loosely "on topic"	Differences and "meaty" answers don't emerge before rapport has been established

Types of introductory questions could include:

Names

Ask what they like to be called.

See if names are spelled correctly on the nametags.

Households

Ask who or what lives at home.

Activities

Ask about interests, passions in life, something they have heart for.

Category usage

Ask about the breadth and frequency of use.

It's helpful to list your introductory questions on an easel for respondents. It's simply more comfortable for some to have a reminder of what they've been asked to share. Others may not need the prompt, but it never hurts.

As a moderator, the introductory questions give you an opportunity to:

- Hear everyone's voice and identify potential concerns (who is soft spoken, who tends to ramble) so that you can address these in a general sense before moving into the topic. (*"Just a reminder—some of you are soft spoken, so for the sake of the tapes I need everyone to bump up the volume a bit."*)

- Make a connection, a virtual thread, between you and each respondent by engaging in a quick back-and-forth verbal exchange. Ask a clarifying or deepening question. If one respondent says he has an iguana, ask *"What's your iguana's name?"* Or if another respondent says that reading is her favorite activity, ask her *"Who's your favorite author?"* Or if someone says he enjoys cooking, ask *"What's your signature dish?"* This enables you to get and give eye contact and nonverbal supporting language. It says you're interested in each respondent as a person. And it sets the stage for future interactions.

Hints

Make sure you give equal attention to everyone. You don't want to give the impression that you find one person more interesting or his or her answers "better" than another's.

Don't get too wrapped up in their answers and don't ask questions that beg for a long-winded response. It is, after all, just the introductory stage. For instance, you don't need to find out the story about how the iguana got its name, especially if the intro question isn't related to your topic. And you don't want to set the model of giving long stories for answers—unless you do, of course. In which case, you might prepare them for this kind of format by saying *"Tell me a story about . . ."* during the intros and allowing enough time for everyone to share.

Variations

Depending upon the type of respondents you've recruited or the tone you want to achieve, you may consider alternative types of introductions. Here are a few you can try:

- When doing friendship pairs or dyads (especially kids), ask them for their favorite dessert or favorite TV show, something that is likely to generate a different answer from each person. As a segue into the discussion, point out the differences you just heard and explain that even friends have different opinions about things and that this is actually what you're looking for in the group discussion. Encourage them to let you know when they agree with each other but also when they have a different idea or response. It's especially important to encourage them to answer what's true for them by assuring them there are no wrong answers.

- When conducting a very diverse group with respect to age, lifestyle, or other characteristics, there will probably be some unifying factor that qualifies them all as participants. But you still may want to use an introductory question that emphasizes commonality. One such activity is to challenge the second person that introduces herself to find something she has in common with the first person. She may need to ask Respondent 1 some additional questions to find similarities, or the group may chime in and help with their observations. The third respondent must find something else she has in common with either Respondent 1 or Respondent 2. Continue around the room. Respondent 1 completes the circle after the last respondent is introduced.

- When conducting a group that will be doing lots of creative or imagery work, ask them as they come into the room to pick a picture from the deck you have on the table—a picture that somehow "speaks" to them. Introductions would then include the basics (name, household, etc.) and then explanations of what they feel the pictures represent in their lives—why these pictures spoke to them.

- There may be times when you want a specific piece of information from participants. You can use their time in the waiting room to your advantage. For example, when doing a group that will be exploring challenges teachers face or needs decision-makers have, ask them to fill out an index card with three wishes, challenges, needs, or problems that they are facing today. This gives them a little private think-time prior to coming into the group. And it allows them to get their own thoughts and perceptions down before hearing what others say. You can use these in the introductions (keeping their answers short and to the point) or save them for a later exercise.

- Ask participants to create their own name cards, illustrated with magazine pictures or symbols that reflect something important about their lives today. Introductions can include describing their name cards.

It's just Not woRking Phil...

QUALITATIVE RESEARCH AND IDEATION
(Or: Fitting a square peg in a round hole)

In the course of planning a qualitative project, has a client ever asked you to allow a little time for respondents to generate ideas around a marketing challenge—maybe a product improvement or a brand extension? More than likely it wasn't the focus of the study, just an add-on. The client probably said something like, "As long as we've got them there, why not ask?" Well, before you jump into it, consider this . . .

Qualitative research is about collecting data, reporting facts, and obtaining reactions. In a nutshell, it's about **what is**. The type of thinking that dominates this process is called "convergent thinking." Convergent thinking is characterized by judgment, evaluation, and deliberation.

Unlike qualitative research, idea generation is about **what could be**. As such, the process for eliciting responses or ideas is quite different. It uses a distinct thinking style known as "divergent thinking," which is characterized by deferral of judgment, proposing the unusual, and striving for quantity. It requires a markedly different atmosphere or environment, one that is uninhibited and playful. And it also requires non-stop techniques to stimulate creativity, as well as significantly more time to accomplish the objective (as much as one or two days). Now does that sound like the thought process and environment of your typical qualitative project? Not our qualitative projects! And it's for these reasons that idea generation in focus groups is, at best, minimally productive and likely to produce only close-in or obvious solutions. At worst, it's a waste of precious interviewing time.

That being said, qualitative research does play an important role in the overall **Creative Problem Solving** (CPS) process, only a part of which is idea generation. An effective problem-solving model—or model for addressing challenges—includes the following broad phases (Parnes, 1981):

- Define the problem or challenge

- Generate ideas or solutions

- Plan for action

Qualitative research can be useful in all three phases of the CPS process. Prior to generating ideas, It's essential to clearly define the problem or challenge. Our motto is, "A problem well-defined is half solved!" Phase one involves collecting data to better understand the current reality—**A STEP THAT'S ESSENTIAL IN DEFINING THE PROBLEM**—and qualitative research is ideally suited to do just that. Phase two includes **BOTH GENERATING NEW IDEAS AND** obtaining reactions to **THEM. QUALITATIVE IS EFFECTIVE IN OBTAINING REACTIONS, BUT NOT IN GENERATING THE IDEAS THEMSELVES.** Finally, qualitative research can also be used to explore the effectiveness of an implemented action plan.

So the next time you're thinking about including idea generation in a qualitative project, think again. More importantly, if obtaining ideas is the primary goal of the project, propose instead a well-crafted session for idea generation.

Suggestions for Using Qualitative When Defining the Problem or Challenge (Phase 1 Of CPS)

Defining the problem or challenge typically requires stepping back and looking at the big picture: people's lives, how they behave, the context in which a product or service is used.

Let's say your client is interested in developing new dinner foods for young families, and in order to understand more clearly the issues to be faced, your client wants to explore dinnertime in busy households with 2.3 children. What could be better than actually watching those lives unfold? Cue the **on-site interviews** (see Chapter 1). Stand in a corner of your respondent's kitchen and watch the meal being prepared, the food being consumed, the kids interacting with the parents. (Learn once and for all who's responsible for hiding the rutabaga!) As households reveal themselves, you'll develop a greater understanding of consumers' lives—their highs, their lows, their delights, their dilemmas. Their needs.

Short of actually going into the home, **storytelling** is a wonderful tool for viewing the big picture (see Chapter 1). Give respondents cameras and have them take pictures of what's happening at dinner and who's doing what to whom. Then have them caption or tell a story about the pictures. Voila! A virtual visit to the family kitchen! **Collages** (see Chapter 3) and written stories work great too—even **drawings** (see Chapter 3). Essentially, give participants the tools and a little direction to construct it, and that big picture will come into sharper focus.

Laddering is also extremely helpful within this context (see Chapter 2). Think about it. The ladder reveals all relevant benefits operative within the existing category, both functional and emotional. Following the dinner foods example, laddering can reveal the ultimate benefits the stakeholder hopes to achieve from the evening meal. Those benefits then become the challenges toward which the ideation is directed, challenges like, how to make meals that *please* both kids and parents; how to make meals *fun*; how to make dinnertime *calm_and relaxed*. (How to get kids to eat rutabaga!) Using challenges like this that are derived from consumer ladders results in product ideas that are driven by actual consumer need. And that's the best kind.

These forms of data collection are incredibly interesting and involving, and they also accomplish the primary goal of supplying the vivid insights necessary to define the problem or challenge prior to launching into idea generation.

A Final Word

(Or: Happy moderating trails!)

So this is it. We've come to the end of the trail, hoping that you are: a) springing out of your saddle, rarin' to go with plenty of ideas for your next project, or b) in a state of minor overload, wondering which direction to take Trigger next! In either case, we'd like to offer a simple guide to help you decide which tools to use and when to use them. Introducing Max's Handy Dandy Trail Map! It's a convenient cross reference of project objectives and tools.

As you're referencing it, remember not to lose sight of your study's overall purpose, and use that as the ultimate driver for selecting any alternative technique. Take it away, Max!

MAX'S HANDY DANDY TRAIL MAP

When you need to learn:	Try using:	Page:
How **alternative points of view** affect attitudes	Hats	120
	Debate	122
Attributes of a product/brand/service that are **important**	Product Sort	22
Comparative perceptions of **before and after** or **reality and wish**	Collage	100
	Drawing	85
	Storytelling	31
Greater/more lucid details about a **behavior, situation, relationship**	Drawing	91
	Mindmapping	14
	On-Site Interviews	51
	Storytelling	31
	Visualization	17
Benefits associated with a product/brand/category	Debate	122
	Laddering	65
	Mindmapping	14

When you need to learn:	Try using:	Page:
How products/brands/services/prototypes **compare on a single attribute/dimension**	Line-Up	25
How products/brands/services/prototypes **compare on a single goal or to the ideal**	Hitting the Mark	29
How products/brands/services/prototypes **compare on two key attributes/dimensions**	Four Square	27
Fit or disconnect of a new product in a line or category	Party/Family of Brands	87
The **frame of reference or competitive set** for a product within a category	Product Sort	22
Imagery, feelings, perceptions about a brand/product/service, issue or experience	Analogy	81
	Collage	100
	Draw the User	109
	Party/Family of Brands	87
	Pass the Doodle	105
	Personification	83
	Picture Decks	94
	Visualization	17
Various **influences** on a decision, perception or issue	Storytelling	31
	Word Bubbles	115
Platforms for idea generation	Laddering	65
Positioning alternatives	Laddering	65
All the **pros and cons** of an issue	Debate	122
Relationship between products in a line or category, or players in a situation	Drawing	91
	Four Square	27
	Line-Up	25
	Party/Family of Brands	87
Sensitive, politically charged or **conflicting** attitudes	Word Bubbles	115
Strengths/weaknesses or **similarities/ differences** relative to competition	Four Square	27
	Line-Up	25
	Product Sort	22
Top-of-mind/incoming attitudes and perceptions of the topic	Free Association	10
	Mindmapping	14
Perceptions of **users**	Draw the User	109

Remember, the closer-in techniques—such as Product Sort and Line-Up—and the metaphorical techniques in which stimuli are provided—such as Picture Sort and Collage—are typically easier for respondents to execute and, as such, can be introduced earlier in the group or interview. While you're still in the experimental stages with alternative techniques, save the more esoteric ones until later, after respondents have warmed up sufficiently and are less likely to glaze over when you ask, "What animal does your favorite morning cereal remind you of?"

What we've outlined above and detailed in the preceding chapters represents our collective conventional wisdom regarding alternative

tools and techniques for use in qualitative research. That said, we encourage you once again to formulate your own conventional wisdom—to adapt these tools, stretch them, morph them. Flex your creative muscles (We knew you had them the moment you picked up this book!), and make them even more effective for addressing your specific objectives and more engaging for your respondents. The tools and techniques in these pages are simply the sparks. You're the one that ignites them!

So now as we ride off into the sunset, saddle up yourself and hit the trails loaded with new ideas and enthusiasm always and above all, Moderating to the Max!

Perceptual Mapping Template
Four Square: Two-Dimensional Continuum

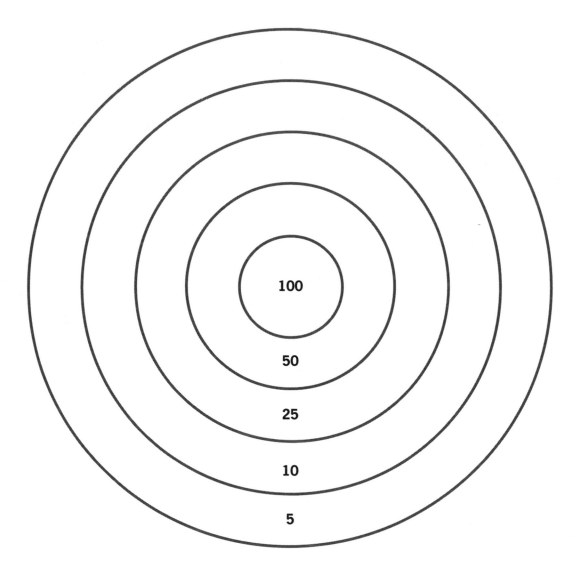

Perceptual Mapping Template
Hitting the Mark: Proximity to the Goal

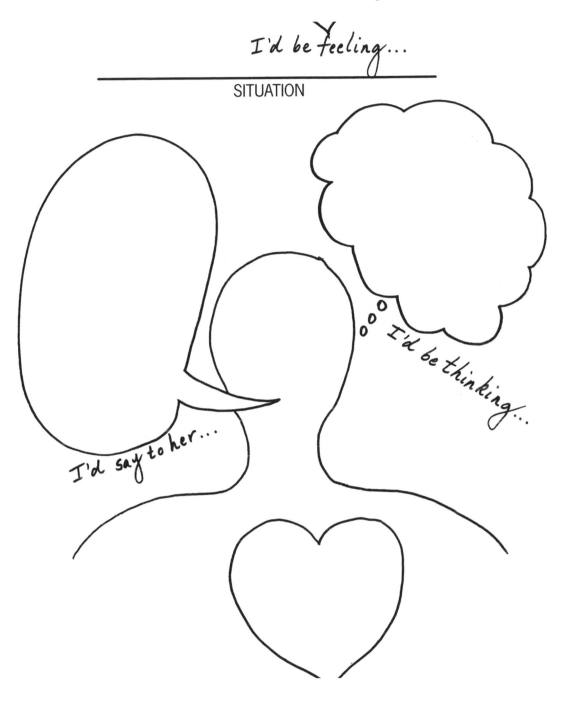

Word Bubble Template: Single View

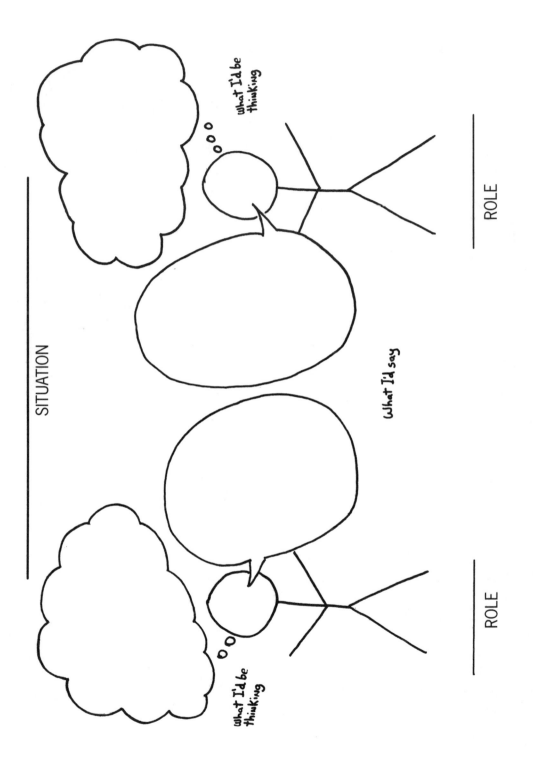

Word Bubble Template: Two Views

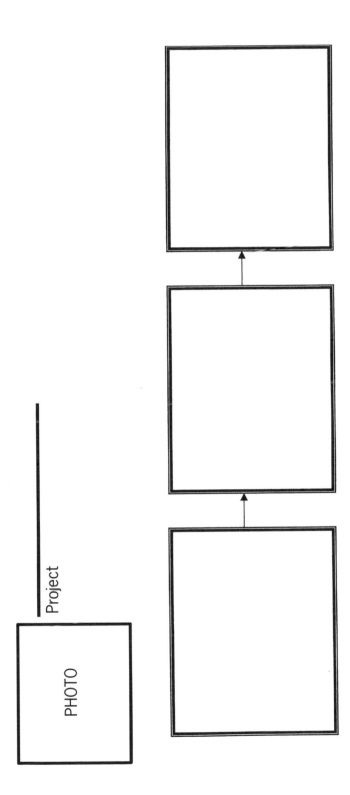

Storyboard Template

References

Bolles, Edmund B. *Remembering and Forgetting: Inquiries into the Nature of Memory*. New York, NY: Walker and Company, 1988.

Bruner, Jerome. *Making Stories: Law, Literature, Life*. New York, NY: Farrar, Straus and Giroux, 2002.

Buzan, Tony. *Use Both Sides of Your Brain*. New York, NY: E.P. Dutton, Inc., 1974.

Bystedt, Jean and Diane Fraley. *Once Upon a Focus Group: Using Storytelling to Capture Consumer Insights*. Presented at QRCA National Convention, 2000.

Gergen, Kenneth J. *An Invitation to Social Construction*. London: Sage Publications, Inc., 1999.

Gobé, Marc. *Emotional Branding*. New York, NY. Allworth Press, 2001.

Goldman, Alfred E. and McDonald, Susan S. *The Group Depth Interview: Principles and Practice*. Englewood Cliffs, NJ: Prentice-Hall, Inc., 1987.

Gordon, Wendy. *The Darkroom of the Mind—What Does Neuro-Psychology Now Tell Us About Brands?* Presented at AQR/QRCA, Paris, 2001.

Gutman, J.. "A means-end chain model based on consumer categorization processes." *Journal of Marketing, 46*, 60–72, 1982.

Jung, Carl G., ed. *Man and His Symbols*. Garden City, NY: Doubleday & Company, Inc., 1964

Kövecses, Zoltán. *Metaphor: A Practical Introduction*. New York, NY: Oxford University Press, 2002.

Langer, Judith. *The Mirrored Window: Focus Groups from a Moderator's Point of View*. Ithaca, NY: Paramount Market Publishing, Inc., 2001.

Maguire, Jack. *The Power of Personal Storytelling: Spinning Tales to Connect with Others*. New York, NY: Jeremy P. Tarcher/Putnam, 1998.

Mariampolski, Hy. *Qualitative Market Research: A Comprehensive Guide*. Thousand Oaks, CA: SAGE, 2001.

Mark, Margaret and Pearson, Carol S. *The Hero and the Outlaw: Building Extraordinary Brands Through the Power of Archtypes.* New York, NY: McGraw Hill, 2001

Parnes, Sidney J. *The Magic of Your Mind.* Buffalo, NY: Creative Education Foundation, Inc. 1981.

Potts, Deborah. *From Native American Mythology to Studs Terkel, the Harvard Business Review to the Qualitative Research Consultant … the Power of Story in Gaining and Communicating Insight.* Presented at QRCA National Convention, 2002.

QRCA. *QRCA Guide to Professional Qualitative Research Practices.* QRCA, Inc, 1997.

Reynolds, Thomas J. and Olson, Jerry C. ed. *Understanding Consumer Decision Making: The Means-End Approach to Marketing and Advertising Strategy.* Mahwah, NJ: Lawrence Erlbaum Associates, 2001.

Robinette, Scott & Brand, Claire. *Emotion Marketing: The Hallmark Way of Winning Customers for Life.* New York, NY: McGraw-Hill, 2001.

Sabena, Pat. *Perceptual Mapping: Where Does My Brand Fit in the Marketplace?* Presented at QRCA National Convention, 1995.

Smith, Jimmy Neil, ed. *Homespun.* New York, NY: Crown, 1988.

Travis, Daryl. *Emotional Branding: How Successful Brands Gain the Irrational Edge.* Roseville, CA: Prima Venture, 2000.

Wycoff, Joyce. *Mindmapping: Your Personal Guide to Exploring Creativity and Problem-Solving.* New York, NY: Berkley Publishing Group, 1991.

The Authors

Siri Lynn, Jean Bystedt, and Deborah Potts, Ph.D. met on the path of professional exploration and growth in the early 1990's. All three are independent qualitative research and creativity consultants who collaborate frequently with one another on strategic marketing and new product initiatives. They are active members of the Qualitative Research Consultants Association (QRCA) and the Creative Education Foundation, senior trainers at RIVA Moderator Training Institute, and leaders at the Creative Problem Solving Institute (CPSI). They are united in a strong desire to contribute to best practices and advance the level of professionalism and innovation within the field of qualitative research.

Siri is the principal of Idea Exchange in Fairfield, CT. When not doing project work, Siri manages to enjoy lots of vacations, social events, and at least one or two classes or conferences a year, all under the guise of challenging and expanding her thinking.

Jean is the principal of J. Bystedt & Associates in Chicago, IL. In her non-business hours she unashamedly indulges in numerous personal passions including: improvising, singing, studying art history, attending theatre, and listening to jazz.

Deborah is the principal of Deborah Potts & Associates, based just outside of Louisville in Prospect, KY. In her spare time, she loves being out-of-doors — hiking, biking, swimming, boating, or just plain walking. She's also making herself at home in Kentucky, attending any bluegrass music event she can find.